Role of Education in Environmental Conservation

Editors

Dr. Mamta Sharma   Dr. Hukam Singh

Dr. Upendra Singh

Pustak Bharati
Toronto Canada

Editors : Dr. Mamta Sharma
Dr. Hukam Singh
Dr. Upendra Singh

Book Title : Role of Education in Environmental Conservation

Cover Picture : By Dr. Anil Kumar Chhangani, D. Sc.

Published by :
Pustak Bharati (Books India)
180 Torresdale Ave, Toronto Canada M2R3E4
email : pustak.bharati.canada@gmail.com
Web : www.pustak-bharati-canada.com

Published for
Raj Rishi Government Autonomous College,
Alwar, Rajasthan, India

Financial Assistance
Rashtriya Uchchatar Shiksha Abhiyan
(RUSA-2.0)

Copyright ©2023

ISBN 978-1-989416-89-1
90000

ISBN : 978-1-989416-89-1

9 781989 416891

Preface

"Our planet is slowly dying, and if we don't do anything about it soon enough, it would eventually begin to deteriorate and everything would be used. The world would become a barren place without any resources. We need to cater to the needs of our planet, and we need to change our life styles so that it becomes beneficial to the planet. We need to become much more eco-friendly, so that no harm is dealt to the planet by our existence. Many people don't realize that they waste large amounts of energy and other resources in various unnecessary things that could otherwise be saved."

This series of books is an extension of the 3 days international conference on **Multidisciplinary Approach Towards Sustainable Development and Climate Change For A Viable Future (ICMSDC-2022)** held from 12th -14th August 2022 at Raj Rishi Government Autonomous College, Alwar, Rajasthan.

We are very happy and delighted to publish our series of books which are accumulation of research papers of knowledgeable experts in the field of sustainable development and climate change.

Climate change is the most significant challenge to achieving sustainable development, and it threatens to drag millions of people into grinding poverty. At the same time, we have never had better know-how and solutions available to avert the crisis and create opportunities for a better life for people all over the world. Climate change is not just a long-term issue. It is happening today, and it entails uncertainties for policy makers trying to shape the future.

There is a dual relationship between sustainable development and climate change. On the one hand, climate change influences key natural and human living conditions and thereby also the basis for social and economic development, while on the other hand, society's priorities on sustainable development influence both the greenhouse gas emissions that are causing climate change and the vulnerability.

Climate policies can be more effective when consistently embedded within broader strategies designed to make national and regional development paths more sustainable. This occurs because the impact of climate variability and change, climate policy responses, and associated socio-economic development will affect the ability of countries to achieve sustainable development goals. Conversely, the pursuit of those goals will in turn affect the opportunities for, and success of, climate policies.

With these books, we aim to reach to as many people as we can, and spread awareness about sustainable development and climate change and its in-depth analysis through our didactic research papers. We hope that the thought with which ICMSDC-2022 was executed is taken forward through this series of books and the inception of an idea of saving the environment is rooted in the minds of our readers.

The articles in these books have been contributed by eminent research scholars, scientists, academicians and industry experts whose contributions have enriched this book series. We thank our publisher, Pustak Bharati, Toronto, Canada for joining us in this initiative and helped in publishing this series of books.

Finally, we will always remain indebted to all our well-wishers for their blessings, without which ICMSDC-2022 and series of these book would have not come into existence.

Financial Assistance provided by Rashtriya Uchchatar Shiksha Abhiyan (RUSA-2.0) is gratefully acknowledged.

Dr. Mamta Sharma
Dr. Hukam Singh
Dr. Upendra Singh

Contents

1. Toxic-Free Environment is Human Right

Dr. Mamta Sharma*,
Dr. Hukam Singh**
Dr. Upendra Singh ***

Introduction

Chemicals are everywhere in our daily life. They form part of nearly all devices we use to ensure our well-being and protect our health Chemicals are the building blocks of the low-carbon, zero pollution, energy- and resource-efficient technologies, materials and products that we need for making our society and economy more sustainable. At the same time, chemicals can have hazardous properties that harm human health and the environment. They can cause cancer, affect the immune, respiratory, endocrine, reproductive and/or cardiovascular systems, weaken human resilience and capacity to respond to vaccines and increase vulnerability to diseases. Consumers are widely exposed to chemicals present in products, from toys and childcare articles to food contact materials, cosmetics, furniture and textiles, to name a few and workers across the world come into contact daily with chemical agents that can be harmful to them. In addition, chemical pollution is one of the key drivers putting the Earth at risk, impacting and amplifying planetary crises such as climate change, degradation of ecosystems and loss of biodiversity. Chemicals, materials and products must therefore become inherently safe and sustainable, from production to end of life, avoiding the most harmful properties and generating the lowest possible impact on climate, resource use, ecosystems and biodiversity.

What is a toxic-free environment and how will we achieve it?

The Chemicals Strategy sets out the steps to take to achieve a toxic-free environment, and ensure that chemicals are produced and used in a way that maximizes their contribution to society while avoiding harm to the planet and to current and future generations. The Strategy foresees that the most harmful chemicals are avoided for non-essential societal use, and that all industrial chemicals are used more safely and sustainably. In parallel, it is equally important to increasingly promote the green transition of the chemical sector and its value chain. A toxic-free environment is part of the Commission's Zero Pollution Ambition for air,

What are examples of toxic chemicals in the environment? How can we prevent further chemical pollution in the future?

So far pollution from chemicals was due to substances that are persistent and have adverse effects on human health and/or the environment, such as polychlorinated biphenyls (PCBs), dioxins, some pesticides (such as DDT) and, more recently, per- and polyfluoroalkyl substances (PFAS). Once a persistent chemical has entered the environment, its effects will continue for a very long period, also when there are no new emissions. The strategy aims to screen chemicals on the basis of their persistency and to act quickly, regulating those that have another property of concern (such as mobility in the environment, bioaccumulation, toxicity). Those substances should only be allowed in uses that are essential for society and if there are no alternatives.

What are substances of concern?

Substances of concern are a group of hazardous substances that are particularly dangerous for human health or the environment, as they cause effects for life. In the context of the Chemicals Strategy, a non-exhaustive list of substances of concern includes those substances identified as of very high concern under REACH as well as those listed in Classification, Labelling and Packaging (CLP) Regulations as having chronic effect on health and the environment. In order to prevent negative long-term effects, the exposure of humans and the environment to these substances of concern should be minimised and substituted as far as possible. The most harmful ones should be especially banned from consumer products and allowed only for proven essential societal use and where no acceptable alternative exist. The development of safe and sustainable by design chemicals and the minimization of these substances in products and waste are key to achieve a clean circular economy.

What is meant by safe and sustainable by design? What are non-toxic material cycles?

Safe and sustainable-by-design means that chemicals, material and processes should avoid from the design phase volumes and chemical properties that may be harmful to human health or the environment, at any stage of their existence. In particular these are groups of chemicals that are likely to be (eco)toxic, persistent, bio-accumulative or mobile. When materials and products are safe throughout their life cycle, from their production to their disposal and recycling, we talk about non-toxic material cycles. Achieving them and transitioning to a clean circular economy implies that the presence of substances of concern must be limited in virgin and recycled materials and that polluted waste is sorted and decontaminated. Sustainability should be ensured by minimizing the environmental footprint of chemicals in particular on climate change, resource use, ecosystems and biodiversity from a lifecycle perspective. The Strategy proposes to define criteria for the overall concept, together with stakeholders.

Is there a link between chemicals in our environment and the COVID-19 pandemic?

Exposure of people to hazardous chemicals weakens our resilience and increases our vulnerability, including to communicable diseases. Chemicals can impact the functioning of the human body in different ways. Of particular importance in the context of the COVID-19 pandemic are chemicals that affect our immune and respiratory systems.

What are endocrine disruptors and in which products do they occur?

Endocrine disruptors are chemical substances that alter the functioning of the endocrine (hormonal) system and, as a consequence, negatively affect the health of humans and animals in different ways (for example by negatively affecting reproductive health or having a role in the development of hormone-related cancers). Some of these substances can be found in everyday products like cosmetics, toys and food packaging. Following the European Commission's Communication (2018) "Towards a comprehensive European Union framework on endocrine disruptors", the Commission and Member States are working on including the identification of endocrine disruptors under the Classification, Labeling and Packaging of chemicals (CLP) Regulation and, in a second step, in the global system (UN Globally Harmonized System). In parallel, we are also working on modifying the REACH annexes to allow the identification of substances as endocrine disruptors.

What is meant by the combination effects of chemicals?

Throughout our lives we are exposed to a variety of chemicals, contained in food, water, medicines, the air that we breathe, and various products. The total risk related to the exposure to a combination of chemicals typically exceeds the risk related to the exposure to each of the individual chemicals on their own. Therefore, exposure to a combination of chemicals can give rise to adverse health and environmental effects, even at levels of exposure that are considered 'safe' for the individual chemicals on their own. Due to the very large number of possible combinations of chemicals, the risk assessment and management of combination effects of chemicals represents a particular scientific and regulatory challenge.

What is the 'one substance, one assessment' and how will it be implemented?

By 'One substance, one assessment' we aim to simplify, streamline and better coordinate the processes that underlie hazard and risk assessments of chemicals, such as initiation of the assessments, allocation of responsibilities for assessments, application of methodologies, use of data and application of transparency rules. The purpose is to improve consistency and quality of assessments across legislation, make more efficient use of expertise and resources, reduce burdens on stakeholders and increase their trust in the scientific underpinning of the assessments. It also aims for faster and more predictable decision-making.

Detour :

Chemicals are everywhere in our daily life. They form part of nearly all device we use to ensure our well-being and protect our health

Chemicals are the building blocks of the low-carbon, zero pollution, energy- and resource-efficient technologies, materials and products that we need for making our society and economy more sustainable. At the same time, chemicals can have hazardous properties that harm human health and the environment. They can cause cancer, affect the immune, respiratory, endocrine, reproductive and/or cardiovascular systems, weaken human resilience and capacity to respond to vaccines and increase vulnerability to diseases. Consumers are widely exposed to chemicals present in products, from toys and childcare articles to food contact materials, cosmetics, furniture and textiles, to name a few and workers across the globe come into contact daily with chemical agents that can be harmful to them. In addition, chemical pollution is one of the key drivers putting the Earth at risk, impacting and amplifying planetary crises such as climate change, degradation of ecosystems and loss of biodiversity.

The Chemicals Strategy is to sets out the steps to achieve a toxic-free environment, and to ensure that chemicals are produced and used in a way that maximises their contribution to society while avoiding harm to the planet and to current and future generations. The Strategy must ensure that the most harmful chemicals are avoided for non-essential societal use, and that all industrial chemicals are used more safely and sustainably. In parallel, it is equally important to increasingly promote the green transition of the chemical sector and its value chain. A toxic-free environment should be the part of the Zero Pollution Ambition for air, water and soil. The solution is making products safe and sustainable by design that has the potential to improve product safety, prevent pollution, mitigate climate change and enable a circular economy.

The term "environmental toxin" evokes only man-made pollution, but naturally occurring substances can be just as harmful. Cyanobacteria (blue-green algae) are toxic to humans, as are some animal venoms, mushrooms, and molds. Arsenic, a naturally occurring element that is widely distributed in the Earth's crust, has many practical applications; it can be found in wood preservatives, pesticides, feed additives, and materials used to make car batteries and semiconductors. Arsenic is also highly toxic. In large enough amounts, it can damage vital organs and cause death. Environmental toxins are substances and organisms that negatively affect health. They include poisonous chemicals and chemical compounds, physical materials that disrupt biological processes, and organisms that cause disease. The effects of exposure to environmental toxins are countless. Major threats include carcinogens, as well as substances affecting cardiovascular, endocrine, and respiratory functions. *Chemicals can enter the environment from many different sources such* as landfills, incinerators, tanks, drums, or factories. Toxic pollutants can poison drinking water, the fish in rivers and ponds, food grown on contaminated farmland, as well as playgrounds, homes, and the very air we breathe. So if you live at a polluted site, you could be exposed to these poisons every time you eat, drink, wash, play or breathe. Environmental toxins are unavoidable. They are in the food we eat, the water we drink, the air we breathe, and many household items we use every day. Largely invisible, most go undetected and are harmless if exposure is limited. However, growth in industrial manufacturing, fossil fuel consumption, and chemical-intensive crop production has dramatically changed the scale and complexity of humans' exposure to environmental toxins, which can carry health risks ranging from mild skin irritation to deadly illness. environmental toxins pose to public health is not as simple as identifying harmful substances and eliminating them. Many of the products and processes contributing to environmental pollution are integral to modern life, and efforts to limit their use are challenged by a lack of research into their effects and by powerful economic forces.

Toxins and Industrialization

Though environmental toxins cannot be neatly categorized as organic or synthetic, the correlation between the increasing threat of toxins and industrialization is undeniable. Dangers associated with any given toxin are largely factors of amount and exposure, and industrial processes have fundamentally changed both. Dangerous amounts of arsenic were once limited to natural concentrations in rocks and soil, but humans now face additional risk of exposure from synthetic arsenic and arsenic waste from coal-burning power plants and mining and smelting operations.

The ubiquity of plastics and other synthetic materials, large-scale application of fertilizers and pesticides necessary for industrialized agriculture, the pharmaceutical industry as we know it — all are relatively new. These products have introduced a multitude of chemicals into the environment, and their effects on humans are incredibly complex and largely unknown.

While our understanding of the toxic effects of modern chemicals is incomplete, some of the dangers associated with industrialization are well established. The World Health Organization estimates that outdoor air pollution accounts for more than 4 million deaths annually due to stroke, heart disease, lung cancer, and chronic respiratory diseases. Major sources of air pollution include the burning of fossil fuels such as coal and oil in industrial production, the operation of motor vehicles, waste incineration, and building heating.

Environmental Chemicals
- Acrylamide.
- Cotinine.
- N,N-Diethyl-meta-toluamide (DEET)
- Dioxin-Like Chemicals.
- Disinfection By-Products (Trihalomethanes)
- Environmental Phenols. Benzophenone-3. Bisphenol A (BPA) Triclosan. 4-tert-Octylphenol.
- Fungicides and Herbicides. Sulfonylurea Herbicides.
- Metals. Arsenic. Cadmium. Lead. Mercury.

Hazardous Substances
Hazardous substances (like fireworks and gasoline) can cause major damage in the event of an accident. Furthermore, emissions of chemicals to air and water can cause long-term negative effects for human health or the environment. People also come into contact with chemicals by using pesticides, cleaning agents or paints, for example.

Fireworks
Fireworks are an example of an explosive substance that can cause major damage in residential areas. Around New Year, many consumers buy fireworks to set them off in their town or

neighborhood. Strict rules apply to the transport, storage and selling of fireworks in built-up areas.

Responsibility for Risks Associated with Hazardous Substances

Responsibility for the risks associated with hazardous substances is divided among a number of authorities :

- Public safety and transport of hazardous substances, rules for placing chemicals on the market and rules for emissions of substances: Ministry of Infrastructure and the Environment.
- Safety at enterprises that work with hazardous substances; Ministry of Social Affairs and Employment;
- Safety of consumer products, cosmetics, food contact materials and toys: Ministry of Health, Welfare and Sports;
- Safety situation in the vicinity of high-risk enterprises: local and provincial authorities. They are obliged, among other things, to ensure that environmental permits comply with requirements for public safety and emissions.

Requirements and Criteria for Environmental Permits

With regard to prevention of accidents, the Hazardous Substances Series (PGS) provides local authorities and regulators with an overview of regulations, requirements and criteria for:

- drafting general rules;
- issuing environmental permits;
- overseeing workplace safety, environmental safety.

Environmental conservation is a practice that paves the way for protecting the environment and natural resources on the individual, organizational as well as government levels. It has become inherently important to work towards environmental conservation in contemporary times in matters to reduce air, water and land pollution, to restore the ecological balance, to ensure the protection of biodiversity and to save our planet from harmful repercussions of global warming. The 7th EAP (EU, 2013) includes a number of chemical-related goals, one of which is that health and environmental risks associated with the use of hazardous substances industry chemicals in products, are accessed and minimized by 2020. While the production and subsequent use of chemicals provides benefits to society, exposure to the hazardous chemicals emitted along the chemical life cycle generates significant risks to health and eco systems. Human exposure to chemicals is associated with a number of disease outcomes, while chemical pollution degrades air and water quality and can impact ecosystem services negatively. The regulation on the registration, authorization and restriction of chemicals (REACH) (EU, 2006) aims to improve the protection of human health and the environment from the risks posed by the chemicals. Chemical control helps to reduce the exposure to hazardous chemicals, thus saving lives and reducing illness and the costs of health care. Chemicals control has the potential to protect the health of both workers and the general population, as it ensures that relevant safety information is made available.

References :
Source of knowledge is the internet and it is highly acknowledged.

*Associate Professor (Zoology)
**Professors
***Associate Professor (Chemistry)
Raj Rishi Government (Autonomous) College Alwar,
Rajasthan ,India.
email : mamta810@gmail.com ;
drhukamsingh63@gmail.com ;
dr.usingh09@gmail.com

2. Town Cultural Library : A Survey

Mr. Kishor Pandharinath Bhole

Abstract

Present paper focuses on the role of Town Cultural library as community information centre in the development of rural masses in various areas such as educational, cultural, socio-economic, agricultural and political, and to know the present status of the Town Cultural libraries and information centre in rural communities. Paper also highlights the services should be provided by the Town Cultural library as community information centre.

Keyword : Town cultural Library Asoda, Rural community.

Introduction

India is a villages based country. Today's Approximately 75% to 80 % total population lives in village. Economies of the country are rolled on village based Agricultural goods which controls Gross domestic product of the country. Rural communities of India has varied need to be information literate on various issues like day-to-day problems, market, health, civics, political, credit, academic, farm inputs, agricultural husbandry practices and international news but there is no institution from where rural communities may get information. In this respect library and information center like Government and Non-Government Public Libraries, Union Information Center, Community information centre and Mobile Libraries can play a vital role. Hence, the purpose of this paper is to discuss the role of information centers to promote and empower the rural communities of India.

The Town library are Public library. "The public library is a practical demonstration of democracy's faith in universal education as a continuing and life long process in the appreciation of the achievement of humanity in knowledge and culture. It is the principle means whereby the record of man's thoughts and ideas and the expression of his creative imagination are made freely available to all. It is the concerned with the refreshment of man spirit with the provision of books for relaxation and pleasure ... and provision of up to date technical, scientific and sociological information."

The achieve these objectives, the Town public library service should be organized with the following essential features –

a. It should be maintained wholly from Town public funds and no direct charge should be made to anyone for its service.
b. It must be readily accessible and its doors should be open free and equal use by all members of the community regardless of area, colour, nationality, age, sex, religion, language status or educational attainments.
c. It should be established under the clear mandate of law, so framed as to ensure nation-wide provision of public library service.

In short a Town cultural public library is one which is authorized by legislation, open to the public without charge and financed out of public funds.

Objectives :

1) To Improve Reading habits of the citizen's of the Asoda with the help study materials.
2) To focus the role of library and information centre in development of rural communities in India.

Research Methodology :

Research Methodology is a way to systematically solve the research problem. It may be understood as a science of studying how research is done scientifically. it is necessary for the researcher to know not only the research method but also the methodology.

The present study is entitled "Town Cultural Library Asoda : A survey" The method to be followed is implied in title itself. The survey method plays significant role in research. The survey method is one of the most effective and sensitive instrument of research, survey research can produce much needed knowledge. "Survey researches approaches through the method of Personal Interviews, Mailed questionnaires and Personal Discussion besides indirect and investigation.

Scope of the Study :

The scope of present study is limited to recognized Town Cultural Public Libraries under the Maharashtra Public Act.1967 in Jalgaon District.

Researcher has selected the subject "Town Cultural Library, Asoda :A Survey". It will fill the gap in our knowledge f public libraries in Asoda.

History of Region :

In fact it is the eastern part of Khandesh, Khandesh by itself was known in 10/12 century A.D. it constituted apart of saunadesa under the YADAVAS and later with the advent Muslim it come to be known as Khandesh.

Today Asoda village isa near of Jalgaon city. Population is a nearly 20000 to 25000 peoples. Here a three primary school, one secondary school, one Junior college. One national bank and two co-opratives banks are available.

Most Important Asoda village of poetss Saint Bahinabai Chaudhari and Saint Zenduji Maharaj.

Town Cultural Libraries and Information Literacy :

The nature of a public library is different from other libraries. Its user community is very different and varied. Their needs for information literacy do not share a common background. Each demand is different from another. So the information literacy services will have to be accordingly flexible to be effective and meet the needs of all the user groups. A representative list of the different user groups may include the following :

a. Senior citizens
b. Children
c. Women
d. Visually challenged
e. Indigenous people
f. Unemployed persons

Town Cultural Library Committee :

1) There shall be Town Library Committee for each district library system in the state which shall be constitute accordance with such rules and regulationsas may be framed by the director in constitution with the council or as by the by laws.

2) The Town Library Committee shall to the approval director as advised by the council frame it's Roll of business and procedure for carrying out the purpose of districts library system.

12

The present study entitled " Town Cultural Library, Asoda : A Survey" is undertaken with a view to have a clear picture of the development and services of the library under study.

Functions of Library :

The UNESCO manifesto has described the role of public libraries in following words –

"The public library must offer to adults and children the opportunity to keep in touch with their times, to educate themselves continuously and keep abrest of progress in the services and arts. His contents should be a living demonstration of the evolution of knowledge and culture, constantly reviewed kept up to date and attractively presented. In this way, it will help people from their own opinions and develop their critical capacities and powers of appreciation. The public library is concerned with the communication and ideas, whatever the form in which these may be expressed."

The for fold function of town cultural Public Library may be elaborated here for a better understanding of its scope of service.

A. Education :

As an educational centre, the public library has to support and promote all types of education formal, non formal, adults and life long by keeping adequate stock of books and other reading materials and making them available to all sections of the community.

B. Culture :

Promotion of culture has two aspects, first reading and thinking develop faculties for aesthetic appreciation, widens mental horizon and develop creative capacities of the individuals. Suddenly, the public library has to contribute to the cultural enrichment of the lectures, seminars, symposium, conferences, book exhibitions and cultural programme.

C. Information :

The scope of information services of a Public library is no longer confined to the provision of traditional reference service to the users, it is extended to include information on other socio-economic needs of the society. A public library has to serve as an information centre or referral contact of a rural public library, employment opportunities, public utility services, facilities provided by the development departments are considered to be the essentials areas of information which may be collected and stored for dissemination to the general public.

D. Recreation :

Provision of scope for healthy recreation of positive use leisure is an important function of a public library. Books of function, magazine, newspaper etc. facilitate recreational reading. Audiovisual materials such as films, increase the utility of a public library. Various forms of performing arts may also be organized in library premises to make them real community centre.

It is necessary to have clear conception of the objectives and roles of public library while organizing such as services for the community.

Resources of Libraries :

Referring to the resources of public library the UNESCO Public Library Manifesto status that –

The public library is concerned which the communication of information ideas, whatever the form in which these may be expressed. Since the printed word has been for the communication of knowledge, ideas and information, books, periodicals and newspapers remain the most important resources of public libraries but science has created new forms of record and these will become an increasing part of the public libraries stock, including print in reduced form for compact storage and vedio tape, for adults and children with the necessary equipment for individuals use and for cultural activities.

1) Books :

The Total books collection of Town Cultural Library, Asoda surveyed was 9492 books.

Knowledge is power and libraries are the resources of this power, this power should never be kept unused, rather it is meant to enlighten the personality of the individual. This power is contained in books in the form of kinetic power.

The library implies the class collaboration of the trio. i.e. the books, the readers and the staff. In fact the books are basic material with which the readers are tp be fed. The books have a pivotal position in the library world, without books there will be no library worth the name.

The books themselves are of various kind and suit various tests and Age groups. Similarly all libraries are not of one kind but are of different kinds and these have to fulfill different purpose. All these makes us select suitable books only.

I. **Adult's Collection** :

In the Town Cultural Library, Asoda. Nearly 25 to 30 % was in adults collection.

a) **Fiction** :

Fiction collection constituted approximately 50 % of total collection in this library. The librarian was asked to rank the types of fiction collection according to their availability, it was found that in this library. Socio-political and historical fiction constituted the largest part of the fiction, largest groups, thrillers ans religious and methodological fiction occupied the next two ranks, there was little experimental and scientific fiction.

b) **Non-Fiction** :

He approximate number of non-fiction books in the Town cultural library, Asoda was 35 % of total collection. In the total adult non-fiction collection history and Biography constitute a major group subject like Art, Sport, Medicine, Science etc. are poorly represented.

II. **Children's Collections** :

Children's from an identifiable group within the community having special needs and interested and for the reason specific library provision must be made to cover the child's need at the Ages and ability levels from infancy to the age of 15 years it is important, however that such provision should be interested physically and administratively with the total public library service. All children's at same time and some children for much of their will need draw to draw on winder resources than those of the children library.

Although children would need to use to use the Adult section providing separate resource for children is an important responsibility of a public library. The total number of children book in 5% in this library.

2) **Periodical** :

It must be noted that the Maharashtra Public Act rules requires 50 titles of periodicals is necessary, Most of Indian and mostly Marathi language subscription are available in library.

3) News Paper :

News Paper cover the matter at different levels. i.e. local, regional, state, national newspaper are the source of up to date news and feature, articles of all the readers interested library purchasing 11 newspaper daily.

Resources in Different Language :

i. **Marathi collection :** On further examination of Marathi collection in various or large. it was observed that 60% to 70% books, periodicals, news paper collection of Marathi language.

ii. **English collection :** The English Language collection extremely limited books, periodicals and news paper.

iii. **Hindi collection :** The Hindi Language collection extremely limited books, periodicals and news paper.

iv. **Urdu collection :** In Asoda village there area better population of Muslim region.only one libbrary in Asoda village. The Urdu language collection is nearly 3% to 5% 0nly.

User's :

1) The Age of user's surveyed was as follows

Sr No.	Age Group users	Number	%
1	Under 16 years	70	17.5
2	16 to 25	170	42.5
3	26 to 40	80	20
4	41 to 60	50	12.5
5	60 and above	30	7.5
	Total User	400	100

2) The following table shows the number of users and frequency of their visit to the Library.

Sr No.	Frequency of visit	Number	%
1	Daily	200	50
2	About twice a week	140	35
3	Once a week	20	5
4	Fortnightly	20	5
5	Once a month	20	5

For the 400 users surveyed more than 50 % users visited the library daily since more than 50% users had stated that they visited the present libarary to read news paper or periodicals.

Conclusion :

The study shows that Town Cultural Library, Asoda have a great role to play . It is important of senior citizen, women's rearder, child user of this library The people of the village are increasing in Agriculture knowledge , current affairs, educational, political, science and other various knowledge all types users are happy as they are getting good facilities through this Town cultural Library.

References :

1) Chopra h.s.,Library Information Technology in modern era.
2) En. Wikipedia.org.
3) Jain Gopal Lal, RuralDevelopment,Mangal deep Pub. Jaipur.
4) Karale Gangadhar, Gramin vikasacha Ekatmik drushtikon, shri mangesh prakashan, Nagpur, ed. I, 2006.
5) Pati M.V., Interdsciplinary Approches to Sustainable Rural Development : Issues and challenges, October 2016.
6) Sadhu A.N., Research Methodology in social sciences.
7) Annual Report Town Cultural Library, Asodain year 1990 to till year.
8) Youna P.V. scientific social survey and Research.
9) Maharashtra Govt., Maharashtra public libraries recognition for grant in aid building ad equipments grants rule 1970.

Dhanaji Nana Chaudhari Vidya Prabodhinis
Loksevak Madhukarrao Chaudhari College of Social Work
Jalgaon, Maharashtra
email : bholekishorp@gmail.com

3. To Study the Flexibility of Maharashtra State Junior Level Volleyball Player

Kunal Vilas Chavan*
Dr. Thakur Rahul Roshanlal**

Abstract

The purpose of this study was to study the flexibility of Maharashtra state junior level male volleyball player. It was a descriptive survey study, in which 96 junior level male volleyball players age of 14 to 18 years were selected as sample from all the participated teams in the Maharashtra state junior level volleyball championship, held at Jalgaon. Each subject was evaluated for flexibility of different body region. The sit & reach, shoulder & wrist and Bridge up flexibility test were used to measure flexibility of lower back & hamstring, shoulder & wrist and abdominal & back flexibility. Data was subjected to statistical treatment like mean, standard deviation and Pearson correlation coefficient in order to find out most significantly correlated flexibility test for junior level male volleyball player. Statistical analysis of the data occur from flexibility tests indicate that, there was significant relationship between sit & reach flexibility test and shoulder & wrist flexibility test (p=0.001). But there was not any significant relationship between sit & reach flexibility test and bridge up flexibility test (p=0.583). And there was also negative significant relationship between shoulder & wrist flexibility test and bridge up flexibility test (p=0.001). At the concluding we can use either sit & reach or shoulder & wrist flexibility test to measure the flexibility of volleyball player.

Keywords : Flexibility, Sit & Reach, Shoulder & wrist, bridge up _

Introduction

In present era, physical education and sports is an essential part of education. It contributes directly to development of physical competence and fitness. It also helps the youth to be aware of the worth of leading a physically active lifestyle. The healthy and physically active youth is more likely to be academically motivated, attentive, and promising. In other words, we can say that physical

18

education and sports is exclusive to the school core curriculum. It is the only programme that provides the opportunities to youth to learn motor skills, progress mental and physical fitness. The benefits of physical gained from physical activity such as disease prevention, safety and injury avoidance, decreased morbidity and premature mortality, and increased mental health.

Physical Education Programme Physical education curriculum can offer youth with the appropriate knowledge, skills, behaviours, and confidence to be physically active for life. Moreover, physical education is the basis of a school's physical activity programme. In the same vein, participation in physical activity is correlated with academic advantages like improved concentration, memory, and classroom behaviour. According to World Health Organization (2001), it includes development of physical abilities and physical conditioning; motivating the students to continue sports and physical activity; and providing recreation activities.

Development of Physical Abilities and Physical Conditioning Physical education facilitates to build up and practice physical fitness entails basic motor skills (Barton et al. 1999) and gets hold of the competency to perform various physical activities and exercises. Physical fitness builds mentally sharper, physically comfortable and also able to deal with the day-to-day demands (Jackson, 1985). Further, endurance, flexibility, strength and coordination are the key components of physical fitness. Moreover, to execute the physical exercises and sport, youth must be developed basic motor skills.

Motivating the Students to Continue Sports and Physical Activity Teachers always motivate the youth to contribute in sports and physical activities as well as academic education programmes. Further, they always direct and instruct them, sports and physical activity are vital part of academic education. They have also guided the youth; we cannot think wholesome development of human personality without sports and physical education. Moreover, they have also to manage a meeting in which discusses their parents about the importance of sports and physical activity as well as academic education. Further, teachers must engage parent or family members in physical activity, for example, by giving youth physical activity 'homework' which could be performed together with the parent's viz., family walks after supper or playing in the park (WHO, 2001).

Providing recreation activities Institutions must focuses on implementation of physical activity course which facilitate to make enjoyable participation to all youth in physical activity programme which provides the youth with a collection of ideas for active games and activities and the skills and fitness to play them (Fox and Harris, 2003) in order to reduce the stress, anxiety, drug abuses and obesity. Promoting the Social Values among Youth Physical education and sports play a vital role in promoting the social values among the youth. Moreover, physical education is considered as a school subject, which facilitate to prepare the youth for a healthy lifestyle and focuses on their overall physical and mental development, as well as imparting important social values among the youth such as fairness, self-discipline, solidarity, team spirit, tolerance and fair play (Bailey, 2005).

Objectives of the Study

1. To measure shoulder & wrist, abdominal & back and lower back & hamstring flexibility of Volleyball players.
2. To find out the correlation between tests for Volleyball.
3. To find out most significantly appropriate flexibility test for Volleyball.

Limitations

The major limitations of this study are that day to day life style, daily physical activity and Socio-economic status of the players

Delimitations

➤ The subjects will be taken from the Maharashtra state only.
➤ The study will be delimited for junior level Volleyball players.
➤ Only male players will be selected for the present study.
➤ Only shoulder & wrist, abdominal & back and lower back & hamstring flexibility will be measured with the help of Shoulder & wrist, bridge up and sit & reach flexibility tests for the present study.

Methodology

This is descriptive co relational study. The researcher is used sits & reach, shoulder & wrist and bridge up flexibility tests for collecting the data. With the help of collected data correlation between each test has been calculated with the help of Descriptive statistics & Spearman co-relation coefficient statistical tools and it helps to find out the most significantly correlated flexibility test for Volleyball.

Data Collection Tools

Test Name	Body Part	Measure
Sit & Reach	Lower back & Hamstring	Lower back & Hamstring flexibility
Shoulder & Wrist	Shoulder and Wrist	Shoulder and Wrist flexibility
Bridge up	Abdominal and Back	Abdominal and Back flexibility

Procedure of the Study

To find out most significantly co-related flexibility test for junior level Volleyball players. The shoulder & wrist, bridge up and sit & reach flexibility test were administered on all 96 players from 8 zone teams namely Amravati, Aurangabad, Kolhapur, Latur, Mumbai, Nagpur, Nashik, Pune, which participated at the junior state level Volleyball championship, held at Jalgaon. Co-relation between each test was calculated. The test which shows high significant co-relationship with other test would be identifying as a significantly relevant test for Volleyball players.

Analysis of Data

The obtained results were presented in below tables which represents the result of descriptive analysis and correlation. The obtained results were presented in the table no.1 and table no.2. which represents the results of descriptive analysis and co relation.

Table No.1
Descriptive Statistics

	Mean	Std. Deviation	N
Sit & Reach	23.08	8.221	96
Shoulder & Wrist	33.33	8.313	96
Bridge Up	52.22	13.932	96

The Sit & Reach, Shoulder & Wrist and Bridge Up flexibility tests were administered on 96 subjects. The mean of sit & reach was 23.08 (± 8.221), shoulder & wrist was 33.33 (± 8.313) and the mean of bridge up was 52.22 (± 13.932).

Table No.2
Correlations

		Sit & Reach	Shoulder and Wrist	Bridge Up
Sit & Reach	Pearson Correlation	1	.321**	-.057
	Sig. (2-tailed)		.001	.583
	N	96	96	96
Shoulder and Wrist	Pearson Correlation	.321**	1	-.336**
	Sig. (2-tailed)	.001		.001
	N	96	96	96
Bridge Up	Pearson Correlation	-.057	-.336**	1
	Sig. (2-tailed)	.583	.001	
	N	96	96	96

**. Correlation is significant at the 0.01 level (2-tailed).

Correlation between sit & reach flexibility test and shoulder & wrist flexibility test 0.321 which was statistically significant at 0.05 significant level (p=0.001).

Correlation between sit & reach flexibility test and bridge up flexibility test -0.057 which was not statistically significant at 0.05 significant level (p=0.583).

Correlation between shoulder & wrist flexibility test and bridge up flexibility test -0.336 which was statistically negative significant at 0.05 significant level (p=0.001).

Discussion and Conclusion

In this present study the researcher found that, there is significant relationship between sit & reach flexibility test and shoulder & wrist flexibility test but there is not any significant relationship between sit & reach and flexibility test and bridge up flexibility test, and there is also negative significant relationship between shoulder & wrist flexibility test and bridge up flexibility test. It means, we can say that those volleyball players are good flexible in lower back & hamstring they also good in shoulder and wrist, but they are not good in abdominal and back flexibility.

References :
1. Al Scates / Mike Linn, Complete conditioning for Volleyball, Human   Kinetics, The premier publisher for Sports & Fitness
2. Sigi S., Complete conditioning for Soccer., The Premier Publisher for Sports & Fitness
3. Sing A., Essential of physical education., publication, New Delhi.

*Director of Physical Education
SMT. N.N.C. ACS. College, Kusumba,
*Director of Physical Education & Research Guide
VES's Sarvajanik Arts College, Visarwadi.

4. Business Growth with Environmental Sustainability

Divya Kirodiwal

Environment refers to the total planetary inheritance. It subdivided into two further elements such as biotic elements and abiotic elements. The environment is surrounding in which we live. A clean environment is essential for the peaceful and healthy survival of humans. Human activities negatively affect the environment. It includes pollution, global warming, deforestation, extinction of species etc.

Sustainable development aims to promoting the kind of development that minimizes environmental problems and meets the needs of the present generation without compromising the ability of the future generation to meet their own needs.

Commerce is keen to anticipate and to respond to consumer demand, working to cut emissions, recover and recycle waste and reduce overall environmental impact, while still offering range, choice and affordability. Protecting the environment is imperative part of business ethics.

Nowadays we see big companies plant trees on the roadside and write their respective organization's name. why do they do so? This is all comes in part of CSR or corporate social responsibility. Doing that gives them cognizance from the locals, which will help them boost goodwill for protecting and contributing to the enviroment's gradation.

Corporate social responsibility or impact on society is a form of self regulation business model, which aims to contribute to social goals such as nature activist, philanthropic, ethical responsibilities towards society. It helps a company be accountable itself to society. Companies can be take responsibilities having all aspects of society, including economic, social, and environmental. To engage in CSR means that, in the routine business, a company is operating in ways that raise society and the environment instead of contributing negatively to them. CSR helps both improve various aspects of society as well as promote a positive brand image of companies in society.

As for superficial attempts to practice CSR, the term "green washing" gives an instance of how the aims of CSR are subverted. **Green Washing refers to the practice of the corporate spin employed by a company in declaring itself to promoting environmentally friendly** policies. It is when an organization spends more time and money on marketing itself as environmentally friendly than on actually minimizing its environmental impact. Simply put, greenwashing is selling your brand as a champion of carbon neutrality and community engagement when it's not. Some of the tactics brands use when they greenwash include rebranding, changing the corporate logo, making claims that can't be measured or marketing themselves as "green" when they're not. The recent past has seen some high-profile instances of greenwashing, including in June 2021, Earth Island Institute filed a lawsuit against Coca-Cola for false advertising—the company had been advertising itself as an eco-friendly and sustainable organization, even though Break Free from Plastic had named Coke the largest plastic polluter four years in a row, including 2021.

Green business model, which ensuring revenue with minimizing the company's environmental impact instead of maximizing its profit. This term covers new and more environmental friendly ways to conduct business.

Now a days, the term "green business model" use. A green industry business is one that uses sustainable materials to make its products. Green industry businesses aim to use as little water, energy and raw materials as possible while cutting carbon emissions, or it finds ways to utilize these materials in renewable and eco-friendly ways.

This business approach minimizes the company's strain on natural resources and contributions to positive climate change.

Lets take a example, if waste is generated, it is reused as energy or raw material or by product.

Now it's a high time that commerce committed to sustainable development of the environment, constantly adapting to the new production and consumption patterns to minimize the environmental impact to produce environmentally friendly products. Business entities need to take the step in solving the environmental issues. It is the responsibility of the company's management to check the outcomes of their actions which requires them to protect environmental resources. A sincere commitment by the top management of the companies to manage, maintain and develop the work culture for environmental protection and for pollution prevention. Companies can developing policies that clearly define programs in order to save the environment which includes disposal and waste management strategies, promoting green energy which reduces the use of fossil fuels. Also, businesses can arrange workshops where training is given and information is being shared along with the experience to get the customers and the suppliers involved in the pollution control programs.

How do businesses go about "greening" their supply chains? A green supply chain or sustainable network could be defined as the operational management method and optimization approach to reduce the environmental impact along the life cycle of the green product, from the raw material to the end product. This term refers to the idea of integrating sustainable environmental processes into the traditional supply chain. For one, they can focus on **using EVs or Electric Vehicles** to transport their goods between the places of production and sales. Let us see how this works and why this does reduce carbon footprints.

As EVs do not emit carbon, since they use electric power to run, unlike Oil guzzling trucks and trailers, businesses can use EVs as a means of greening their supply chains. Considering the fact that transportation forms the major (if not entire) component of the supply chain, using EVs can be a "game changer" for businesses trying to be Net Zero compliant.

Another way of turning your supply chain into a green and sustainable, in the process of packaging materials, some of the packaging are done with containers made of plastic. Businesses should work on minimizing the use of plastic and switch to packaging made from sustainable materials. This will help in the reduction of plastic as well as boost eco-friendly materials.

Another way to reduce negative impact on environment is to switch present business process with environment friendly manner. Businesses can generates electricity from solar energy. It means that company uses less fossil fuel, reducing pollution and greenhouse gas emissions.

By switching to solar power, companies' does its part to fight climate change and to reduce country's dependence of foreign energy sources. But the benefits go further- being a sustainable business can not only reduce your operating costs, but can also built positive public relations. Research shows that a growing number of consumers make their buying decisions based on companies' environmental responsibility.

Another way to boost business while also improving the environment. **"green building practices"** is very good example of it. A "green" building is a building that, in its design, construction or operation, reduces negative impacts, and can create positive impacts on our climate and natural environment. Green buildings preserve precious natural resources and improve our quality of life. Sustainable buildings minimize energy and water consumption. It enhanced air quality and excellent day-lighting and provides healthier space for occupants. This idea has the greatest potential to reduce CO_2 emissions. Currently, 30% of global CO_2 emissions and 40 % of global resource consumption is a result of constructing buildings. The built environment has a vast impact on the natural environment, human health, and the economy. By adopting green building strategies, we can maximize both economic and environmental performance. Experience has shown that investing in green infrastructure can contribute to healthier economy by fostering in innovative approaches and creating new green businesses. Also green job market is a very grown in future aspects. Green building has created millions of jobs and contributes in economy development. Green building concepts benefits to operating cost savings, shorter payback periods and increased asset value in new green buildings. Also investment in green building also makes properties more valuable, with a growing number of building owners. Green buildings reduce day-to-day costs. Reports says that almost 20% lower maintenance costs than typical commercial buildings, and green building retrofits typically decrease operation costs by almost 10% in just one year.

Here, we discuss a story of a successful business organization. Pretty sure you know the company "Reliance". What crosses your mind when you hear of this company? Telecom, petroleum, refinery etc. this is the story of reliance and mangoes.

Before I tell you what it has to do with mangoes, let's back to 1997. One of the biggest weakness of Reliance at that time was the huge amount of pollution in Jamnagar refinery. The pollution control boards, Reliance convert the wastelands of Jamnagar into a mango orchard near the refineries as a way to control pollution.

Fast forward to 2018, that orchard, now known as "Dhirubhai Ambani Lakhibag Amrayee' is Asia's best mango orchard with more than 1.3 lakh plants of over 200 species. The mangoes produced in that orchard are of excellent quality and are widely exported at a global level. Reliance grows 127 varieties of mango in a 600-acre green belt at its Jamnagar refinery complex.

This is a great example of how we can turn our weakness into our strengths. We can grow our business by taking the environment along without harming the environment, because business cannot progress by destroying nature. Business and industry avail the resources from the environment. "Environment is the path on which only business can achieve its objectives". Therefore, it is important for every individual and business entity to save and protect our environment.

References
1. Management study guide
2. Business Magazine- "Fortune"
3. John Kaler- 2003- Journal of Business Ethics
4. Indian Journal of Industrial Relations Vol.44, No. 3, CSR

5. Newspapers- "The Dainik Bhaskar", "The Hindustan times", "The Economics times"
6. Environmental protection agency, "Location and Green Building," March 19, 2017

Student,
Baboo Shobha Ram Govt. Arts Collage, Alwar
Rajasthan
email : divyakirodiwal96@gmail.com

5. The Effects of The Image of Destination on Tourist Satisfaction in Varkala

Dr. M. Gayathiri [1]
Ms. G. Subapriya [2]
Ms. Harini [3]

Abstract

One of the most significant sectors of the world economy is tourism. Worldwide, it creates millions of employment and billions of dollars in revenue. Many communities, particularly in developing nations, view it as the only resource for development and the only opportunity to improve the standard of living. However, at the same time, the darker aspect of tourism began to emerge. Visitors' and investors' actions both have a detrimental effect on the socio-cultural values and environmental resources of host communities around the globe. In this essay, we attempt to examine how tourism affects society from three angles: fiscal, social and cultural, and environmental.

The economic benefits of tourism include higher tax collections and individual incomes, rising living standards, and more job possibilities. Influences include attitudes and behaviors, relationships to material possessions, and interactions between individuals from different cultural backgrounds. The development of public policy should also priorities projects that are supported by governments and foreign organizations as well as the corporate social responsibility initiatives of tourism businesses in local communities.

Keywords : Tourism, Satisfaction, World economy, Developing nation.

Introduction

Without blowing smoke, tourism is the largest business in the world. One in nine employments worldwide is held by it, and it accounts for 10% of the global GDP. It is an area of external economic activity that is rapidly expanding. It has an impact on various other economic sectors due to its rapid growth and development, significant inflows of foreign money, expansion of the infrastructure, and introduction of new management and educational opportunities. Consequentially, it contributes favorably to the overall social and economic growth of the nation. It has amazing real and potential economic effects. In this paper, the economic effect of tourism on India is thus attempted to be quantified. There are currently many ways to gauge the effect. The crucial measurements are the multiplier method, the input-output method.

Impact of Tourism - Overview

Both good and negative effects of tourism are felt in popular tourist areas. Economic, socio-cultural, and environmental dimensions are the traditional categories used to characterize the impacts of tourism. The economic benefits of tourism include higher tax collections and individual incomes, rising living standards, and more job possibilities. influences include attitudes and behaviors, relationships to material possessions, and interactions between individuals from different cultural backgrounds. Degradation of habitat, vegetation, air quality, water bodies, the water table, wildlife, and changes to natural phenomena are examples of direct environmental impacts. Indirect effects include increased harvesting of natural resources for food, indirect air pollution, and changes to natural phenomena (including from flights, transport and the manufacture of food and souvenirs for tourists).

For locals, tourism has both beneficial and detrimental effects on their health. The short-term detrimental effects of tourism on locals' health are associated with the volume of visitors, the danger of disease transmission, traffic accidents, higher crime rates, as well as crowding, congestion, and other stressful circumstances. Furthermore, residents may experience anxiety and depression as a result of their risk perceptions regarding mortality rates, food insecurity, interaction with infectious tourists, etc., which may have a negative impact on their mental health. The improvement of healthcare access, positive feelings, novelty, and social interactions are some of the beneficial long-term effects of tourism on locals' health and well-being.

Review of Literature

Dr Kawal Gill in their article entitled, "The vast majority of the tourism literature concentrates on how locals perceive the industry because it is locals in host communities who are directly impacted by the presence of tourism in the area". Little scholarly attention has been paid to this exclusive focus on residents' perceptions, which is intended to advance the conceptual understanding of how tourists perceive and evaluate tourism effects on their visiting locations. In reality, the region's overall tourism development needs to give just as much consideration to how visitors perceive the area. Visitors appear to have an extensive variety of options for what they can do and cannot do that could affect how their visits will affect society, the economy, and the environment both separately and collectively. Naturally, these can be both good and bad. Consequently, there is a strong argument.

Fernanda Strozzi his study analyzed that, "A quantitative bibliometric analysis was carried out using software tools and algorithms, allowing us to dynamically depict the flow of knowledge development over time. In order to provide a comprehensive picture of the state of the art and the research trajectories of the knowledge on tourism and its economic effect, we combined the results of such analyses. Furthermore, the main path analysis proved to be very helpful in locating the foundational works of each area of study due to the breadth and heterogeneity of all the related topics about tourism.

Three is the main section of Tolga Savas study, which infers the environmental effects of the tourism business. This study investigates this issue by contrasting and comparing two locations in the world with a history of nefarious behavior. This paper examines a subtype of dark tourism that we call "fright tourism" because some visitors may be looking for a rush or a surprise. Particularly, a visitor will look for a chance at a location that might have a sinister past or is being advertised as having one.

Objetives of the Study

➢ To know the level of satisfaction of the Tourist in Varkala
➢ To ascertain the factors effecting the level of satisfaction toward

tourism in Varkala

Methodology

Both Primary and Secondary data form the basis of the study. Primary data was collected with the help of Interview Schedule. Secondary data was obtained from bulletins, brochures, articles, web collections, reference books, newspapers and publications of Tourism department. The study area covers tourist place of Varkala in Kerala. 25 tourists were selected to express their views by adopting convenient sampling technique. The data was analysed using Simple Percentage Analysis and Chi-Square Test.

Limitations of the Study

- This study is on the basis of the opinion given by the tourists in Varkala.
- The information given by the respondents may also be unfair.
- The respondents are selected by employing convenient sampling method and the limitationsare related to it is applicable.

Findings of the Study

Level of Satisfaction

Satisfaction index is computed to know the Satisfaction level of the respondents in Varkala. Tourism in Varkala provides various benefits to all tourists. Seven factors are considered for the present study. The response is rated on a five point scale. Answer to the questions range from one to five. Thus, the maximum score will be 35. The Mean Satisfaction is 64 and Standard deviation is 11.19. The score up to 53.15 is categorized asLow, the score from 53.16 to 75.52 is categorized as Medium and the score above 75.53 is categorized as High.

TABLE 1: Satisfaction level of Tourist

Level of Satisfaction	Number of Respondents	Percentage
Low	5	20.00
Medium	16	64.00
High	4	16.00
Total	25	100.00

Source : Primary Data

Out of 25 tourists, 5 (20.00 per cent) are having low level of Satisfaction, 16 (64.00 per cent) holders have medium level of Satisfaction and 4 (16.00 per cent) respondents are with high level of Satisfaction on the services provided by Tourism. It is found that majority of the respondents are with medium level of Satisfaction.

Variables Influencing the Satisfaction Level of Tourist

The following hypothesis is framed to find out the variables associated with the Satisfaction factors:

H_0-There exists a significant association between the select variables and level of Satisfaction.

TABLE 2: Variables associated with the Satisfaction factors

Variables	Level of Satisfaction						Total n=25	df	χ^2 Value
	Low		Medium		High				
	n=5	%	n=16	%	n=4	%			
Nationality									
Indian	0	0.0	6	60.0	4	100.0	10		
German	1	25.0	3	75.0	0	0.0	4		
Russian	2	40.0	3	60.0	0	0.0	5	8	0.080
European	2	66.7	1	33.3	0	0.0	3		
Newsland	0	0.0	3	100.0	0	0.0	3		
Gender									
Male	3	21.4	9	64.3	2	14.3	14	2	0.955
Female	2	18.2	7	63.6	2	18.2	11		
Age									
Less than 18	1	50.0	1	50.0	0	0.0	2		
18 - 35	2	18.2	9	81.8	0	0.0	11	6	0.158
36 - 50	1	10.0	5	50.0	4	40.0	10		
Above 50	1	50.0	1	50.0	0	0.0	2		
Marital Status									
Married	2	10.5	13	68.4	4	21.1	19	2	0.080
Unmarried	3	50.0	3	50.0	0	0.0	6		
Occupation									
Student	1	25.0	3	75.0	0	0.0	4		
Government Service	1	16.7	4	66.7	1	16.7	6		
Professional Service	1	50.0	1	50.0	0	0.0	2	8	0.751
Self Employed	2	25.0	5	62.5	1	12.5	8		
Others	0	0.0	3	60.0	2	40.0	5		

Source: Primary Data

Table 2 reveals that there exists no association between the personal variables- nationality, gender, age, marital status, occupation- and the degree of satisfaction.

Suggestions

➢ Reduce the level of pollution like water, air and noise, etc.
➢ Decrease the process of degradation of local infrastructure and environment. Infrastructure can be modified in a better manner.
➢ Provide most transport services in this area.
➢ Enhance more fun and entertainment activities and display of local art and architecture.
➢ Strict rules should be made to protect the environment.

Conclusion

As a conclusion, we can state that tourism is a very profitable endeavor for both the government and the traveler. They concurrently support one another. Additionally, the government ought to think about enhancing the nation's circumstances as more and more tourists come to the nation. By addressing the empirical evidence regarding the effects of tourism on local communities, this paper contributes in a number of ways. The development of public policy should also prioritize projects that are supported by governments and foreign organizations as well as the corporate social responsibility initiatives of tourism businesses in local communities. As a result, these communities need to have education and training programs that focus on social skills development, tourism industry operations (such as lodging, food, drink, transportation, and guided tours), management, and entrepreneurship.

Referance

➢ Dogan Gursoy, Robin Nunkoo (2019) – The Routledge Handbook of Tourism Impacts.
➢ Kunal Chattopadhyay (1995) – Economic Impact of Tourism Development : An Indian Experience.
➢ Alister Mathieson, Geoffrey wall (1982) – Tourism : Economic, Physical , Social Impacts.

- Peter Nijkamp (2016) – Impact Assessment in Tourism Economics, " This book presents a series of studies on socio-economic impacts of tourism.
- Melhem, S. B.; Albaity, M. (2017) -The viewpoint of international tourists on novelty seeking, image, and loyalty. The mediating role of satisfaction and the moderating role of duration of stay. 23, 30, and 37. Perspectives on tourism administration.
- Gerbing, D. W., and Anderson, J. C. (1988) - Practice of structural equation modelling: A overview and suggested two-step procedure. 103(3):411-423 in Psychological Bulletin.
- Dowling.R. K. (1990) - The transition from idealism to reality in tourism and environmental integration. In Progress in tourism, recreation, and hospitality administration, edited by C. P. Cooper and A. Lockwood. Belhaven, in London.
- DUNCAN, J. H. (1977). - A search for an eclectic strategy to trade, the location of economic activity, and the multinational enterprise. The worldwide distribution of economic activity, edited by B. Ohlin, P. Hesselborn, and P. Wijkman. McMillan, London.

[1]Assistant Professor,
Department of Commerce,
Karpagam Academy of Higher Education, Coimbatore, India
[2] Student (B.Com) & [3] Student (B.Sc Microbiology),
Karpagam Academy of Higher Education, Coimbatore, India

6. SARS-COV-2 Variants of Concern (VOC): Facts about Alpha, Beta and other COVID-19 Mutants

Bhoye S. B

Abstract

Coronaviruses (CoV) are a large family of viruses that cause illnesses ranging from the common cold to severe illnesses such as Middle East Respiratory Syndrome (MERS-CoV) and Severe Acute Respiratory Syndrome (SARS-CoV). A novel coronavirus (nCoV) is a new strain that has not previously been identified in humans. Coronaviruses are zoonotic, meaning they are transmitted between animals and people. Detailed investigations revealed that SARS-CoV was transmitted from civet cats to humans and MERS-CoV from camels to humans. Many known coronaviruses are circulating in animals that have not yet infected humans. Viruses like SARS-CoV-2 change over time and will continue to change the longer they circulate. Sometimes, strains of the virus can develop. One type is where the virus contains at least one new change to the original virus. Viruses constantly change through mutation. When a virus undergoes one or more new mutations, it is called a variant of the original virus. Certain types of coronaviruses, such as alpha, beta, gamma, delta, and omicron, are more easily spread among people.

Keywords : MERS-CoV, SARS-CoV, nCoV, Chronology, Variants

Introduction

The coronavirus (COV) was first discovered in mammals and birds in the 1960s, what do you need to know about the chronology of COV? Because CoV is transmitted from animals to humans. This detailed information on severe acute respiratory syndrome (SARS-COV) transmission from civet cats to humans, Middle East respiratory syndrome (MERS-COV) dromedary camels to humans, several known CoV are human-to-human bloodborne animals, human-to-human transmission, which infects the world's human population. Infection with this CoV causes the respiratory system, fever, cough, shortness of breath and difficulty breathing, more infections such as pneumonia, severe acute respiratory syndrome with kidney failure and death, bronchitis virus in chickens, and infection in the form of two viruses from nasal cavity of human patrub with common cold. That's why we call human coronavirus COV-229E in 1963, human corona OC43 in 1967, other tools of this family are the same as SARS-COV in 2003, H-COV NL63 in 2004, HKU in 2005, MERS-COV. 2012, before SARS COV-2 in 2019-nCOV 2019. Most human coronaviruses are a large family of viruses that cause diseases ranging from the common cold to more severe illnesses such as MERS COV and SARS COV, currently called coronavirus COV 2019-2020 Corona virus is an ongoing pandemic of corona virus disease (n- COVID-19). The COVID-19 virus is caused by SARS COV-2. The 2019–20 coronavirus pandemic is an ongoing pandemic of coronavirus disease 2019 (COVID-19) caused by the severe acute respiratory syndrome corona virus 2 (SARS-CoV-2).[1] These viruses chronology is given in Table 1.

The outbreak of n-COVID-19 was first identified on 01 December 2019 in the city of Wuhan, Hubei, China, and was recognized as a pandemic by the World Health Organization (WHO) on 11 March 2020. [2] At the same time, the "WHO" made a statement that this was the first known epidemic that could be controlled.[2] As of 15 March 2020, more than 157,000 cases of COVID-19 have been reported in about 130 countries and territories; more than 5,800 people have died from the disease and about 75,000 have recovered. [3] Most of the regions affected by major outbreaks include mainland China, Europe, Iran, South Korea, and the United States.[3][4] On 13 March 2020, the WHO stated that European countries are the current epicenter of the epidemic.[5]

The corona virus is mainly spread between people in an influenza-like way, through respiratory droplets from coughs.[6] The time between exposure and symptom onset is usually five days, but can range from two to fourteen days.[6][7] Symptoms often include fever, dry cough, and shortness of breath.[6][7] Complications may include pneumonia and acute respiratory distress syndrome. There is no single vaccine or specific antiviral treatment yet, but research is still ongoing. Efforts are mainly aimed at managing symptoms and supportive therapy, but recommended preventive measures include hand washing, social distancing (especially from strangers), and fourteen days of observation and self-quarantine for people suspected of having such cases.[6][8]

Public health responses include national pandemic preparedness and response plans.[9][10] People are subject to travel restrictions, quarantines, curfews, program postponements and cancellations, and facility closings. These include the quarantine of Hubei in China, the quarantine of both Italy and Spain; Curfew measures in China and South Korea, as well as other countries have been alerted.[11][12] Travel advisories regarding various border closures or inbound travel restrictions, [13][14] screening procedures at airports and train stations,[15] and community spread regions.[16][17] Schools and universities have closed on a nationwide or local basis in at least 61 countries, affecting more than 500 million students.[18] Viruses are always changing and new types or strains of viruses may emerge. A variant usually does not affect how the virus works. But sometimes they work in different ways.

These Viruses' Chronology is given in Table 1.

Coronavirus Genera	First Outbreaks	Earliest Samples	Designated Variant of Concern (VOC)
Alfa (B.1.1.7)	United Kingdom	20Sep 2020 [19]	18 Dec 2020 [21]
Beta (B.1.351)	South Africa	May 2020	14 Jan 2021 [22]
Gamma P.1 (B.1.1.28.1)	Brazil	Nov 2020	15 Jan 2021 [23]
Delta (B.1.617.2)	India	Oct 2020	6 May 2021 [24]
Omicron (B.1.1.529)	South Africa	9 Nov 2021 [20]	26 Nov 2021 [25]

Variants of concern is given in Table 2.

Sr. No.	Variants of concern (VOC)	Characteristics
1.	**Alpha (B.1.1.7)**	First detected in the United Kingdom and designated a type of concern in December 2020.[26] It has several key mutations in the spike protein - which the virus uses to gain entry into human cells - that marks it out from the original Wuhan strain. One is the N501Y mutation, which causes the spike protein to bind to cellular receptors making the virus more infectious. It also contains the D614G mutation, which is thought to increase viral replication, and the P681H mutation, whose function is unclear, but which has arisen several times spontaneously. Alpha is estimated to be about 40-80% more infectious (contagious) than the original Wuhan strain.[27]
2.	**Beta (B.1.351)**	The Beta variant was first detected in South Africa and was also designated a variant of concern in December 2020.[28] In addition to the three mutations found in the alpha (or alpha plus) variants (E484K, N501Y, and D614G), beta has the K417N mutation, which may help the virus avoid neutralizing antibodies elicited by vaccination or previous infection. It is thought to be about 50% more transmissible than the previous types, but there is little evidence that beta is associated with more severe disease. South Africa's Department of Health has also indicated that this strain is causing a second wave of the Covid-19 pandemic in the country as it is spreading faster than other previous strains of

		the virus.[29]
3.	**Gamma (P.1)**	Designated as a species of concern in January 2021, Gamma was first detected in Brazil.[30] Like other forms of anxiety, it has E484K, N501Y and D614G mutations. It also has the K417T mutation - associated with increased binding to human cells, which may make it easier for the virus to spread - and the H655Y mutation, whose function is unknown. Gamma showed 2.2 times higher infectivity with equal ability to infect both adults and the elderly, indicating that P.1 and P.1-like lineages were more successful in infecting young humans regardless of sex.[31]
4.	**Delta (B.1.617.2)**	The Delta variant was first detected in India in May 2021,[32] and quickly overtook existing variants to become the dominant variant in many countries.[33] Delta includes the D614G mutation, as well as many additional ones not seen in other anxiety types. These include the L452R mutation, which is thought to increase infectivity and may help the virus evade immune cell destruction; a T478K mutation, thought to help avoid recognition by the immune system; and a P681R mutation, which is associated with an enhanced ability to trigger severe disease. There have also been reports of a 'Delta Plus' variant, first identified in Nepal and carrying an additional K417N mutation. The delta variant is 40-60% more transmissible than the alpha variant and approximately twice as infectious as the original Wuhan strain of SARS-CoV-2. [34][35]

5.	**Omicron (B.1.1.529)**	Omicron was rapidly identified in several countries in November, 2021,[36] after South African scientists alerted the WHO to a sudden increase in COVID-19 cases in Gauteng province. The first known confirmed Omicron infection was from a sample collected on November 9, 2021. As of December 3, 2021, it has been verified in 22 locations worldwide, including parts of North and South America, Europe, Africa, Asia, and Australia. Omicron has a large number of mutations, some of which are related. These include the N501Y, D614G, K417N and T478K mutations,[37] which are also found in other forms of anxiety, as well as many others that have not yet been described. It is not yet clear whether Omicron spreads more easily from person to person than other types or whether its infection causes more severe disease.[38]

Conclusion :

All viruses, including the Covid-19 virus, mutate over time and this is a natural phenomenon. However, some mutations or combinations can change the behavior of the virus. Viruses change constantly through mutations, and sometimes these mutations lead to new types of viruses. Some types arise and disappear while others persist. New forms will continue to emerge. Delta and Omicron are of concern because they carry a large number of mutations, some of which are associated with potentially increased infectivity and potential immunosuppression. Although there are many similarities between the new COVID-19 and the virus that caused the SARS epidemic, there are also differences due to changes in their genomes.

References :

[1] Gobalenya AE, Baker SC, Baric RS, et. al., (2020). "The species severe acute respiratory syndrome-related coronavirus: classifying 2019-nCoV and naming it SARS-CoV-2". Nature Microbiology: 1–9.

[2] "Coronavirus Disease (COVID-19)., (2020): Events as they happen". www.who.int.

[3] "Threat of coronavirus pandemic 'has become very real': WHO's Tedros". Reuters (2020).

[4] Liptak, Kevin., (2020): "Trump declares a national emergency to combat coronavirus". CNN.

[5] "Europe is now the coronavirus epicentre of the world, says WHO". Evening Standard. (2020).

[6] "Symptoms of Novel Coronavirus (2019-nCoV) | CDC". U.S. Centers for Disease Control and Prevention (CDC). (2020).

[7] Rothan HA, Byrareddy SN (2020): "The epidemiology and pathogenesis of coronavirus disease (COVID-19) outbreak". Journal of Autoimmunity.

[8] "Coronavirus Disease 2019 (COVID-19)"., (2020): Centers for Disease Control and Prevention.

[9] Health, Australian Government Department of (2020): "Australian Health Sector Emergency Response Plan for Novel Coronavirus (COVID-19)". Australian Government Department of Health.

[10] CDC (2020): "Coronavirus Disease 2019 (COVID-19) Situation Summary". Centers for Disease Control and Prevention.

[11] "Coronavirus: Shanghai neighbor Zhejiang imposes draconian quarantine". South China Morning Post. (2020).

[12] Marsh S, (2020).: "Four cruise ship passengers test positive in UK – as it happened". The Guardian. ISSN 0261-3077.

[13] Nikel, David., (2020): "Denmark Closes Border to All International Tourists for One Month". Forbes.

[14] Hermesauto, (2020): "Coronavirus: Poland to close borders to foreigners, quarantine returnees". The Straits Times.

[15] "Coronavirus Update, (2020): Masks and Temperature Checks in Hong Kong". Nevada Public Radio.

[16] "Coronavirus Disease 2019 Information for Travel", (2020): U.S. Centers for Disease Control and Prevention (CDC).

[17] Deerwester J, Gilbertson D. (2020): "Coronavirus: US says 'do not travel' to Wuhan, China, as airlines issue waivers, add safeguards". USA Today. Archived from the original.

[18] "Coronavirus impacts education". UNESCO. (2020).

[19] Rambaut A, Loman N, Pybus O, Barclay W, Barrett J, Carabelli A, et al. (2020): "Preliminary genomic characterization of an emergent SARS-CoV-2 lineage in the UK defined by a novel set of spike mutations". *Virological.*

[20] Callaway, Ewen (2021): "Heavily mutated coronavirus variant puts scientists on alert". *Nature.* **600** (7887): 21.

[21] Investigation of novel SARS-COV-2 variant, technical briefing 1 (PDF) (Briefing). Public Health England. (2020).

[22] Horby P, Barclay W, Huntley C, (2021): *NERVTAG paper: brief note on SARS-CoV-2 variants* (Note). Public Health England.

[23] "Confirmed cases of COVID-19 variants identified in UK". *GOV.UK.* Public Health England. (2021).

[24] *SARS-CoV-2 variants of concern and variants under investigation in England, technical briefing 10* (PDF) (Briefing). Public Health England. (2021).

[25] "Classification of Omicron (B.1.1.529): SARS-CoV-2 Variant of Concern". World Health Organization. (2021).

[26] "Covid: Ireland, Italy, Belgium and Netherlands ban flights from UK". *BBC News.* (2020).

[27] Volz E, Mishra S, Chand M, Barrett JC, Johnson R, Geidelberg L, et al. (2021). "Assessing transmissibility of SARS-CoV-2 lineage B.1.1.7 in England". *Nature.* **593** (7858): 266–269.

[28] "South Africa announces a new coronavirus variant". *The New York Times.* (2020).

[29] Wroughton L, Bearak M, (2020): "South Africa coronavirus: Second wave fueled by new strain, teen 'rage festivals'". *The Washington Post.*

[30] "Japan finds new coronavirus variant in travelers from Brazil". *Japan Today*. Japan. (2021).

[31] Nascimento V, Souza V, (2021): "COVID-19 epidemic in the Brazilian state of Amazonas was driven by long-term persistence of endemic SARS-CoV-2 lineages and the recent emergence of the new Variant of Concern P.1". *Research Square*.

[32] "India says new COVID variant is a concern". *Reuters*. Bengaluru. (2021).

[33] "Delta Globally Dominant Covid Strain, Now Spread To 185 Countries: WHO". (2021).

[34] Mishra, Swapnil; Mindermann, Sören; Sharma, Mrinank; et. al., (2021): "Changing composition of SARS-CoV-2 lineages and rise of Delta variant in England". *EClinicalMedicine*. **39**: 101064. doi: 10.1016/j.eclinm.2021.101064. ISSN 2589-5370.

[35] Bhoye S, Marakwad T, (2021): A Comparative Characteristics of Both Variants of Severe Acute Respiratory Syndrome Coronavirus-2 (SARS-CoV-2): Delta and Omicron. International Journal of Creative Research Thoughts (IJCRT). 9 (12), p838-835.

[36] "Classification of Omicron (B.1.1.529): SARS-CoV-2 Variant of Concern". *www.who.int*. (2021).

[37] Callaway, Ewen, (2021): "Heavily mutated coronavirus variant puts scientists on alert". *Nature*. **600** (7887): 21.

[38] "Covid infections rising again across UK - ONS". *BBC News*. (2022).

**Assistant Professor,
Department of Zoology,
Shri Pundlik Maharaj Mahavidyalaya, Nandura Rly.
Dist. Buldana.
email : Shantarambhoye8@gmail.com**

7. राजस्थान के पर्यटन उद्योग के विकास में राजस्थान पर्यटन विकास निगम की भूमिका का मूल्यांकन

Dr. Manoj kumar Sethia

इस शोध पत्र में प्रदेश के पर्यटन विकास हेतु 1978 में स्थापित राजस्थान पर्यटन विकास निगम की भूमिका का अध्ययन व विश्लेषण किया गया है । राजस्थान पर्यटन विकास निगम ने प्रादेशिक पर्यटन विकास हेतु 2 बातों की आवश्यकता को विशेष रूप से महसूस किया –

(1) प्रदेश में पर्यटन वातावरण का निर्माण करना ।

(2) पर्यटकों को बेहतर सुविधाएँ उपलब्ध करवाना ।

पर्यटन वातावरण के विकास हेतु निगम ने जहाँ आधारभूत ढांचे के विकास पर बल दिया, वहीं दूसरी ओर पर्यटकों को बेहतर सुविधाएँ उपलब्ध करवाने के साथ–साथ शैक्षणिक सुविधाएँ, रोजगार सृजन, सांस्कृतिक एवं अन्य गतिविधियों का संचालन भी समय–समय पर किया जाता है । प्रदेश के पर्यटन विकास में राजस्थान पर्यटन विकास निगम की भूमिका को निम्न प्रकार से प्रस्तुत किया गया है –

• पर्यटन सुविधाओं के क्षेत्र में (आवास, खानपान, बीमा–बैंकिग)

• शैक्षणिक सुविधाओं के क्षेत्र में (पर्यटन साहित्य, प्रशिक्षण, पर्यटन प्रचार–प्रसार एवं विपणन)

• धार्मिक, सांस्कृतिक एवं अन्य गतिविधियों के क्षेत्र में

पर्यटन–सुविधाओं के क्षेत्र में योगदान
आवास व खानपान के सम्बन्ध में

राजस्थान पर्यटन विकास निगम ने प्रदेश मे पर्यटकों की बढ़ती हुई संख्या को देखते हुए जहाँ एक ओर कम दर पर बेहतर भोजन व्यवस्था के लिए बजट होटलों पर विशेष ध्यान दिया हैं, वहीं दूसरी ओर आवास–व्यवस्था हेतु अनेक नवीन कार्यक्रम बना रही है ।

निगम की कुल 75 इकाइयाँ है, जिनमें से 39 होटल, 22 मोटल, 8 कैफैटेरिया, 3 यात्रिकाएं शामिल है । निगम द्वारा संचालित आवास इकाइयों में 964 कमरे तथा 8 डोरमेंट्री कमरे हैं, जिनकी कुल शयन क्षमता 1982 है । निगम द्वारा संचालित 48 इकाइयों में भोजन सुविधाएं एवं 29 में बार सुविधा उपलब्ध है। आवास की पेइंग गेस्ट योजना 27 सितम्बर, 1991 को प्रारम्भ की गई, जो प्रदेश के 13 शहरों में संचालित है ।

पैकेज ट्यूर

राजस्थान पर्यटन विकास निगम समय–समय पर ऐसे आकर्षक पैकेज ट्यूर बनाता है, जिनके माध्यम से प्रदेश के लगभग सभी पर्यटन स्थलों का भ्रमण संभव बनता है । जैसे :

- ऐतिहासिक, धार्मिक, पुरातात्विक महत्व के पर्यटक पैकेज
- रेल रोमांच, साहसिक खेल के पर्यटन पैकेज
- क्रूज यात्रा पैकेज
- ग्रामीण पर्यटन पैकेज

परिवहन

पर्यटकों को बेहतर परिवहन–सुविधा के लिए 26 जनवरी, 1982 को पैलेस ऑन व्हील्स, जनवरी 2009 में 'रॉयल राजस्थान ऑन व्हील्स' ट्रेन प्रारम्भ की गई।

पर्यटक पथ–प्रदर्शक

निगम पर्यटन कार्यों के संचालन की इकाई है, जो पर्यटन गाइडों की गुणवता में सुधार हेतु प्रयासरत है । प्रदेश में महिला व पुरूष–गाइडों में 1.5:98.5 का अनुपात पाया गया । अध्ययन के दौरान स्पष्ट हुआ कि 75 प्रतिशत पर्यटक गाइडों की सेवा से सन्तुष्ट है । अतः निगम को इन सेवाओं को सशक्त बनाने के लिए नये आयामों के साथ प्रभावी प्रशिक्षण की व्यवस्था पर विशेष ध्यान देने की आवश्यकता है ।

बीमा–बैंकिंग–संचार

सुविधाओं के सम्बन्ध में निगम के अधिकारियों से सकारात्मक जवाब नहीं मिलता । अधिकारियों के अनुसार आगन्तुक पर्यटकों को इन सुविधा स्थलों व संस्थाओं के बारे में तो वांछित जानकारी उपलब्ध करवा दी जाती हैं, लेकिन राजस्थान पर्यटन विकास निगम के स्वंय के स्तर पर अभी तक इस प्रकार की सुविधाओं का कोई ठोस आधार विकसित नहीं किया गया हैं। पर्यटकों को मजबूरन निजी संस्थाओं पर निर्भर रहना पड़ता हैं । भविष्य में शीघ्र ही ऐसी सुविधाओं का निगम के स्तर पर शुभारम्भ संभावित हैं ।

सूचना एवं प्रौद्योगिकी

निगम पर्यटन सम्बन्धी सूचनाओं के अन्तर्गत पुस्तिकाओं, ब्रोशर, पेम्पलेट प्रकाशन के साथ–साथ परम्परागत गन्तव्यों, नये परिपथों, अल्पज्ञात क्षेत्रों, विभिन्न पर्यटन केन्द्रों के नक्शे, पर्यटन सम्बन्धी नियमों का प्रकाशन भी करता हैं ।

शैक्षणिक सुविधाओं के क्षेत्र में

हस्तशिल्प

निगम द्वारा प्रादेशिक हस्तशिल्प कला के अस्तित्व, संरक्षण व विकास–संवर्द्धन हेतु हस्तशिल्प कला के पुराने व अनुभवी उद्यमियों को आर्थिक मदद देता है । शोध व अनुसंधान कार्यक्रम करवाता है । दुर्लभ कला–वस्तुओं की

सुरक्षा हेतु संग्राहलय व्यवस्था भी की है । उदयपुर में शिल्पग्राम ही स्थापना की गई है ।

पर्यटन साहित्य

निगम समय समय पर होने वाले मेले, सांस्कृतिक, धार्मिक हलचलों, ऐतिहासिक स्थलों, हैरिटेज होटलों आदि के विषय में पर्यटन साहित्य का मुद्रण व वितरण कता है । चालू वर्ष 2010 में कोलकाता में आयोजित ट्रेवल एवं टूरिज्म फेयर में राजस्थान को **'बेस्ट पवेलियन अवार्ड'** पर्यटन मंत्री सुल्तान अहमद द्वारा **बीकानेर ढोलामारू के सहायक निदेशक हनुमान मल आर्य को दिया गया ।**

प्रशिक्षण

पर्यटन के क्षेत्र में मानव संसाधन विकास हेतु निम्न प्रशिक्षण संस्थान संचालित किए जा रहे हैं :

● होटल प्रबन्ध संस्थान, जोधपुर

● फूड क्राफ्ट संस्थान, अजमेर

● फूड क्राफ्ट संस्थान, उदयपुर

धार्मिक, सांस्कृतिक व अन्य गतिविधियों के सम्बन्ध में

प्रदेश में धार्मिक व सांस्कृतिक पर्यटन को बढ़ावा देने के लिए विभिन्न क्षेत्रों में स्थित मन्दिरों के पर्यटन सर्किट ही नहीं बनाए गए हैं, बल्कि ऐतिहासिक व पौराणिक महत्व के मन्दिरों के जीर्णोद्धार के कार्य हेतु राज्य के बजट में भी विशेष प्रावधान की व्यवस्था है । धार्मिक व सांस्कृतिक कार्यक्रमों की सफल क्रियान्विति हेतु समारोह स्थल पर सुरक्षाकर्मियों की नियुक्ति व्यवस्था, परिवहन व्यवस्था, ठहरने हेतु धर्मशालाओं की व्यवस्था, असामाजिक तत्वों से होने वाली गड़बड़ी की रोकथाम की व्यवस्था भी गई हैं। राज्य के प्रमुख मन्दिरों एवं तीर्थ स्थलों से सम्बन्धित सूचनाओं हेतु एक बेबसाइट (www.rajsthandevasthan.com) भी तैयार करवाई गई है ।

पिछले एक दशक से निगम प्रादेशिक पर्यटन विभाग में निजी भागीदारी पर विशेष ध्यान दे रहा है, जिसके कारण वर्तमान में अनेक ग्रामीण क्षेत्र पर्यटन क्षेत्र के रूप में उभर कर सामन आ रहे हैं, जैसे – उदयपुर का शिल्पग्राम व बीकानेर जिले का कतारियासर ।

आधाभूत सुविधाओं, शैक्षणिक सुविधाएँ, धार्मिक सांस्कृतिक व अन्य गतिविधयों के सम्बन्ध में सुविधाएँ पर्यटन उद्योग के विकास की प्रथम आवश्यकता हैं । इस दिशा में निगम के प्रयास संतोषजनक नहीं कहे जा सकते, क्योंकि –

● महाविद्यालय व विश्वविद्यालय स्तर पर पर्यटन शिक्षा व पर्यटन आधारित रोजगारोन्मुखी कार्यक्रम नाममात्र के संचालित हो रहे हैं ।

● प्रशिक्षण कार्यक्रम पर्याप्त स्तर के नहीं हैं ।

● प्रदेश की अधिकांश जनता भी प्रादेशिक पर्यटन सम्पदा से बिल्कुल अनभिज्ञ है।

- पर्यटक गाइड़ों की सेवाओं से सन्तुष्ट नहीं हैं ।
- आम जन को पर्यटकों से जोड़ने, पर्यटन स्थलों को साफ–सुथरा रखने, पर्यटकों के साथ आत्मीयता से पेश आने, पर्यटकों की समुचित व्यवस्था का अभाव हैं ।

यदि निगम उपरोक्त सुविधाओं की समुचित व्यवस्था कर पाता है, तो वर्तमान पर्यटन आय स्तर को 20–30 प्रतिशत तक बढ़ाया जा सकता है ।

संदर्भ सूची

1. Acharya Ram, World Tourism, National Publication, New Delhi, 2004
2. Akhater Javed, Tourism Management in India, Ashish Publication House, New Delhi, 2000
3. Anand, Uma, Guide to India, ITDC Delhi, 1995
4. Breden John M., Tourism and Development, Cambridge University Press Cambridge, 1993
5. Bright, M.G., Financial Management : Tata McGraw Hill Publishing Co. Ltd., New Delhi, 2004
6. Bringham E.F., Financial Management, The Dryden Press Hinsdale, llinois Ed. 2004
7. Burkat A.J., The Management of Tourism, Henni Man, London, 2005
8. C.R. Kothari, Research Methodology Methods and Techniques, Wiley Eastern Limited, New Delhi, 1998
9. Choudhary, S.B., Management Accounting, Kalyani Publishing, Ludhiyana, Ed. 1996
10. Derbvin, E.F.M., Method of research-A-Plea for Co-operation in Social Science in Economics, 1998

Assistant Professor
SBJS Rampuria Jain College Bikaner
Manojsethia82@gmail.com

8. Role of Teachers in Imparting Education for Environmental Preservation

Masarrat Sultana

Abstract

The air we breathe, the water we drink, the land we live upon, the soil we use to build our houses and the fruit and vegetables we eat, all comes under nature. Nature is providing us with tremendous amounts of natural resources. *Exploitation* of *natural resources* is an essential condition of the human existence; overexploitation is leading to depletion of natural resources and environmental degradation. The dawn of the industrial era has harmed nature and its resources which were randomly exploited for many decades without restoring the earth to its natural state. Teachers are considered to be the most important members of our society. Teachers are the ultimate role models for students. Teachers should sensitize their students on various alarming environmental problems. Teachers should take active part in creating awareness through environmental education. The teachers should be trained and make them educated for creating awareness among new generations. It is the duty of teachers to identify the correct ways and means for educating and preparing the students for sustainable environmental education that requires the cooperation of society as well. Among these is the use of curriculum by teachers to impart knowledge to protect and preserve environment for sustainable development. There is no better way to inculcate respect for nature than to encourage learners to spend some time with nature, organizing small cleaning events of areas, introduce students to recycling and arrange seminars, celebration of important days, debates, preparation of models etc. They should also encourage students to go green, plant trees, protect wildlife and to act as a green warrior for preservation of environment and sustainable development.

Keywords : Teachers role, Environmental Education, Preservation, Sustainable development

Introduction

There is lack of environmental awareness about preservation and conservation which usually leads to degradation of the environmental quality .If such situation continues in the near future, the entire planet will face disastrous situation. At this point the important thing is to create environmental awareness among the people young generation and all the people regarding protection, preservation and conservation of environment which can be done by environmental education.

Environmental education is a process that allows individuals to explore environmental issues, engage in problem solving, and take action to improve the environment. As a result, individuals develop a deeper understanding of environmental issues and have the skills to make informed and responsible decisions. Environmental education helps students understand how their decisions and actions affect the environment, builds knowledge and skills necessary to address complex environmental issues, as well as ways we can take action to keep our environment healthy and sustainable for the future. *Environmental education* empowers individuals, groups and institutions to properly explore environmental issues along thoughts and activities for environmental conservation. Environmental education provide every person with opportunities to acquire the knowledge, values, attitudes, commitment and skills needed to protect and improve the environment; to create new patterns of behavior of individuals, groups and society as a whole towards the environment. Today as you know one of the best places to nurture environmental awareness is inside the classroom with teachers discussing different environmental issues. Today's students can be tomorrow's stewards of nature. So, they need a firm understanding of the many environmental issues and problems that need to be addressed and a clear grasp of what it will take to deal with them. Some of these important issues include climate change, global warming, air pollution, poor management of waste, growing water scarcity, falling groundwater tables, water pollution, preservation and quality of forests, biodiversity loss, and land/soil degradation, overpopulation, resource depletion, solid waste generation are some of the major environmental issues that are putting a tremendous strain on the planet and its finite resources. A Study on Level of Environmental Awareness among College Students in Coimbatore District was carried out by Priya (2014). Saladie and Santos-Lacueva(2016) studied the role of awareness campaigns in the improvement of separate collection rates of municipal waste among university students a causal chain approach. Theories and concepts for human behavior in environmental preservation were reported by Akintunde (2017). Bakri etal.(2017) conducted a survey on awareness and attitudes of secondary school students regarding plastic pollution : implications for environmental education and public health in Sharjah city , UAE . Tangwanichagapong etal.(2017) showed greening of a campus through waste management initiatives experience from a higher education institution .Goldman etal.(2018) reported influence of 'green school certification' on students' environmental literacy and adoption of sustainable practice by schools. Das and Pitale (2018)studied environmental awareness through education. Liao and Li (2019) studied environmental education, knowledge, and high school students' intention toward separation of solid waste on campus. Boca and Saraçlı(2019) studied environmental education and student's perception for sustainability .Investigating students' sustainability awareness and the curriculum of technology education in Pakistan was studied by Malik (2019). Whitburn etal. (2019) reported exposure to urban nature and tree planting are related to pro-environmental behavior via connection to nature, the use of nature for psychological restoration, and environmental attitudes. Ardoin etal (2020) made a systematic review on "Environmental education outcomes for conservation. Bashir etal(2020) studied appraisal of student's awareness and practices on waste management and recycling in the Malaysian University's student hostel area.Chauhan and Gihar (2020) studied effect of non-formal environmental education activities on primary school students environmental awareness. Umer Abdela (2020) conducted a review on school based environmental club impact on student and general environment. Barcelo-Oliver (2021) conducted scientific activities for the engagement of undergraduate students in the separation and recycling of waste. Qu and Shevchenko (2021) carried out advancing waste management program at university in China: enlightenment from the Netherlands .Chandran and Azeez (2022) conducted Environmental education in the schools of Coimbatore district, Tamil Nadu. Role of teachers in environmental education among school children was reported by Pandey etal.(2022).Panzo etal.(2022)carried out a case study in Angolan secondary schools related to Environmental awareness on solid waste management practices.

Environmental Awareness

Environmental awareness is having an understanding of the environment, the impacts of human behaviors on it, and the importance of its protection. Environmental awareness is critical because it can help to minimize pollution and global warming. It can also lead to a more sustainable world by promoting renewable resources such as solar, wind, and water. *Environmental awareness* involves understanding and appreciating the natural world and the challenges we face in protecting it.

Environmental awareness *can promote the need for a healthy environment which brings pollution less surrounding*. The environment awareness education lays emphasis on certain crucial points as alertness, location, conservation skill and sustainable development etc. Alertness includes making the person conscious about the physical, social and aesthetic aspects of the environment.

Non formal education includes organization of extra-curricular activities like eco development camps, posters and essay-writing competitions, exhibitions, seminars, nature camps, nature-club activities, audio visual slides, museums, nature centers, zoos or parks, mobile exhibitions etc.

Role of Teachers

Considering a prodigious role in education system, the role of teacher is very important in nation building and also has a valuable role to play in conservation, preservation and spreading environmental awareness amongst the students. A teacher is regarded as the friend, philosopher, and guide of the student. Teacher can play an important role in educating their students related to environmental protection and preservation which is possible only when the teacher themselves have the necessary level of environmental education awareness. The role of teacher is to help the children as well as illiterate adults to know, to protect and to enrich the environment. Traditionally, teacher has been regarded as an agent of social change and modernization. Every individual has the responsibility to protect our environment, but students are considered to be unique because they will be the future of our planet. Students can make the earth a better place. Environment belongs to each one of us and all of we have a responsibility to contribute towards its conservation and protection. A teacher therefore can play an important role in providing environmental awareness and developing a positive attitude towards environment among students by the following ways :

1. Helping students to acquire knowledge related to environment
2. Create awareness regarding natural resources
3. Making the students aware of different environmental issues
4. Creating awareness regarding the ways for protection and preservation of the environment
5. Developing eco friendly habits amongst students
6. Participating the students in various programmes related to environmental preservation
7. Motivate the students to acquire social moral and ethical values regarding protection and preservation of the environment
8. Helping the students in every possible way and conduct skits and street plays on environmental conservation
9. Helping them to learn the solutions for solving environmental problems
10. Organizing visits to polluted industries, polluted rivers, zoos, national parks, wild life sanctuaries etc.
11. Organizing seminars, workshops on environmental issues like soil erosion, population explosion, pollution, global warming, climate change, deforestation, depletion of natural resources, biodiversity and other related issues etc.
12. Organizing lecture talks by the eminent resource personalities of their respective field of expertise
13. Planting trees , formation of eco clubs, ban on polythene bags

14. Motivating the students to enhance their knowledge by watching programmes related to environment
15. Awareness regarding reuse, reduce and recycle the things for protection and preservation of the environment
16. Celebration of important days like World water day, World earth day, World environment day World forest day, Wildlife week, World ozone day etc. should be made a practice
17. Awareness regarding no driving day, asking them to walk, cycle or take a train or bus instead of the private car or bike
18. Banning on plastics and utilization of jute or cloth bags
19. Educating students regarding segregation of wastes and composting process
20. Awareness regarding switching of electric devices when not in use
21. Educate and create awareness for environmental preservation with the help of research activities
22. Motivating the students to use renewable sources of energy
23. Utilization of eco friendly products

Sustainable Development

Sustainable development is defined as development that meets the needs of the present without compromising the ability of future generation to meet their own needs. The onus of protecting the environment for the present and future generations also rests with human beings alone. Environmental sustainability is one of the biggest challenges faced by human beings on this planet due to large amount of manmade activities and even over utilization and exploitation of our natural resources. The aim is to protect our planet and environment and do stop these practices can be considered to start from students. Therefore teachers have to play an important role in educating and shaping the students for protecting and preserving our environment.

Conclusion

Therefore, we can say that environmental education is a process directed at creating awareness and understating about environmental issues that leads to responsible individuals. A teacher can play an important role in creating environmental awareness. So he/she must educate to his/her students regarding various issues and problems related to environment and motivate them to acquire the skills of solving environmental problems. It is very essential that students should be educated by trained teachers regarding the ways of protection and conservation of the environment. This will then inculcate among the students sensitivity towards environmental issues and will positively develop a responsible attitude towards the environment. To achieve a good quality of life on this planet earth for all human beings, it is very essential to spread awareness about and educate humankind for sustainable development and environmental problems. The conservation and preservation is related to the individuals effort to save and protect the environment.

References

1. Akintunde E A.(2017): Theories and concepts for human behavior in environmental preservation. J. Environ. Sci. Public Health.;1(2):120–133.
2. Bakri M., Hammami A., Mohammed E.Q. (2017) Survey on awareness and attitudes of secondary school students regarding plastic pollution : implications for environmental education and public health in Sharjah city , UAE. Environ. Sci. Pollut. Control Ser.;24(25):20626–20633.
3. Bashir, M.J.; Jun, Y.; Yi, L.; Abushammala, M.F.; Abu Amr, S.S.; Pratt, L.M. (2020)Appraisal of student's awareness and practices on waste management and recycling in the Malaysian University's student hostel area. *J. Mater. Cycles Waste Manag.* *22*, 916–927.
4. Barcelo-Oliver, M.; Cabello, C.P.; Torrens-Serra, J.; Miro, M.; Cabot, C.; Bosch, R.; Delgado, M.R. (2021) Scientific activities for the engagement of undergraduate students in the separation and recycling of waste. *J. Chem. Educ.*, *98*, 454–460.
5. Boca, G.D.; Saraçlı, S. (2019) Environmental Education and Student's Perception, for Sustainability. Sustainability, 11, 1553

6. Chandran R. and P.A. Azeez(2022) Environmental Education in the Schools of Coimbatore District, Tamil Nadu Eco. Env. & Cons. 28 (4): pp. (1743-1753)

7. Goldman D., Ayalon O., Baum D., Weiss B. (2018) Influence of 'green school certification' on students' environmental literacy and adoption of sustainable practice by schools. J. Clean. Prod.;183:1300–1313

8. Kamlakar Prasad Pandey Sunita Wathre and Sandeep Pandey (2022) Role of teachers in environmental education among school children IRJEdT Volume: 04 Issue: 11: pp.137-143

9. Liao, C.; Li, H. (2019) Environmental education, knowledge, and high school students' intention toward separation of solid waste on campus. *Int. J. Environ. Res. Public Health* , *16*, 1659.

10. Muhammad Noman Malik , Huma Hayat Khan, Abdoulmohammad Gholamzadeh Chofreh , Feybi Ariani Goni , Jiˇrí Jaromír Klemeš and Youseef Alotaibi(2019) Investigating Students' Sustainability Awareness and the Curriculum of Technology Education in Pakistan Sustainability, 11, 2651; doi:10.3390/su11092651

11. N.M. Ardoin, A.W. Bowers and E. Gaillard(2020) Environmental education outcomes for conservation: A systematic review. Biological Conservation, 241, 108224.

12. P. Chauhan and R. Gihar R(2020) Effect of Non-formal Environmental Education Activities on Primary School Students Environmental Awareness", ZENITH International Journal of Multidisciplinary Research, 10(12), , pp 59-68.

13. Priya, K. (2014) A Study on Level of Environmental Awareness among College Students in Coimbatore District. Online International Interdisciplinary Research Journal. 4: 391-394.

14. Qu, D.; Shevchenko, T. (2021) Advancing waste management program at university in China: Enlightenment from the Netherlands. *Bull. Sumy Natl. Agrar. Univ. 3*, 54–65.

15. Saladie, O.; Santos-Lacueva, R. (2016) The role of awareness campaigns in the improvement of separate collection rates of municipal waste among university students: A causal chain approach. *Waste Manag. , 48*, 48–55

16. Subhash Das, Priyanka Pitale (2018) Environmental Awareness through Education International Journal of Advances in Science Engineering and Technology, ISSN(p): 2321 –8991, ISSN(e): 2321 –9009 Volume-6, Issue-4, Oct.-2018, http://iraj.in
17. T.I. Panzo, J.C. Góis, J.M. Mendes(2022) Environmental awareness on solid waste management practices: A case study in Angolan secondary schools. J Civil Eng Environ Sci, 8(2), pp 076-081.
18. Tangwanichagapong S., Nitivattananon V., Mohanty B., Visvanathan C. (2017) Greening of a campus through waste management initiatives Experience from a higher education institution. Int. J. Sustain. High Educ.; 18(2):203–217.
19. Umer Abdela (2020) Review on School Based Environmental Club Impact on Student and General Environment .Civil and Environmental Research ISSN 2224-5790 (Paper) ISSN 2225-0514 (Online) Vol.12, No.6
20. Whitburn J., Linklater W.L., Milfont T.L. (2019)Exposure to urban nature and tree planting are related to pro-environmental behavior via connection to nature , the use of nature for psychological restoration , and environmental attitudes. Environ. Behav; 51(7):787–810.

Professor,
Shreeyash College of Engineering and Technology, Aurangabad
Maharashtra
email : drmasarrats@gmail.com

9. Role of Human Rights in Protecting the Environment

Deepika Singh

Abstract

For decades, man's endless desire to achieve economic development has adversely impacted mother nature. Over-exploitation of natural resources, population explosion, uncontrolled and unplanned industrialization and urbanization have led to excessive environmental degradation. The resulting environmental problems such as pollution, global warming and climate change, ozone layer depletion and loss of biodiversity are being realized world over. Our environment has degraded to such an extent that the various species inhabiting this planet are now bearing the brunt of mankind's irresponsible actions. The present environmental crisis needs to be handled with a collective approach wherein all human beings acknowledge the fact that a clean and healthy environment is a fundamental right to each one of us. If we intend to protect our environment, then we must first safeguard the basic human rights as the two are closely inter-connected. The right to a healthy environment, already recognized as a basic human right by the United Nations, must be constitutionalized by all countries and additional laws should also be enacted to ensure its protection. By doing so, the environment is also protected, and the goal of sustainable development can be achieved wherein development on this planet proceeds in a way that the quality of life of every human being is improved with minimum damage to the environment. This ensures that the future generations also have access to a clean and healthy environment. The paper reviews the efforts made by the United Nations establishing the importance of basic human environmental rights and the role they play in environmental protection. It also lists the efforts made at the level of various states, with special reference to India. Lastly, it highlights the fact that environmental rights hold value only when duties of protecting and preserving the natural environment are performed well.

Keywords : environment, protection, fundamental, healthy, human right.

Introduction

In present times, environmental degradation has become a major problem faced by the whole world. The natural resources on this planet, comprising of both living and nonliving components, are now depleted at faster rates. Unorganized human activities are mostly responsible for the deteriorating changes in the availability and quality of natural resources. For instance, in China, growing urbanization has influenced both environmental and human health. (Zhu et al., 2011) Similarly, findings suggest that population growth contributes towards the decline in the environmental quality. (Khan et al., 2021) All types of environments, whether air, water and soil are increasingly getting polluted, thus intensifying environment related health risks. The *Lancet* Commission on pollution and health reported that pollution resulted in 9 million premature deaths in 2015, making it the biggest environmental risk factor for disease and premature mortality in the world. (Fuller et al., 2022)

Pollution also indirectly hinders a country's economic growth. A World Bank report estimated that the cost of the health damage caused by air pollution amounts to $ 8.1 trillion a year, equivalent to 6.1% of global GDP. (World Bank Group, 2022) Air pollution is related to climate change. Burning of fossil fuels and emissions from diesel-fueled vehicles release pollutants such as methane, hydrofluorocarbons and tropospheric ozone which are more significant contributors to climate warming than carbon dioxide. (*Climate Explainer: Climate Change and Air Pollution*, n.d.) The adverse impacts of environmental pollution and climate change are largely faced by poor and vulnerable sections of society. There is an urgent need to empower them with rights that would help them claim a clean, safe and healthy environment for their survival and existence.

United Nations Contribution towards Environmental Rights :

In the past few decades, various attempts have been made both at the international and national levels to specify the significance of human rights in relation to the environment. The 1972 United Nations

Conference on the human environment in Stockholm was the first such attempt to recognize the relationship between human rights and the environment. Principle 1 of the Stockholm declaration states that "Men has the fundamental right to freedom, equality and adequate conditions of life in an environment of a quality that permits a life of dignity and well-being and improve the environment for present and future generations." (*Report of The United Nations Conference on The Human Environment. Stockholm 5-16 June,1972. A/CONF./48/14/Rev.1*, n.d.) Stockholm conference also resulted in the establishment of UNEP (United Nations Environment Programme) which has since then played an important role in addressing environmental problems and supporting sustainable development.

Men has wrongly used the power of science and technology resulting in serious harms to the environment. Despite the various efforts made to achieve economic and social development, millions of people continue to suffer due to poverty and are deprived of a clean, safe and healthy environment, which is their basic right. Any development should be planned in a way to ensure the protection of environmental rights. Such development will be in harmony with nature and in the right direction of achieving the goal of sustainability. In 1992 the United Nations Conference on Environment and Development (UNCED) took place in Rio de Janeiro. It is also known as the Earth Summit. The Rio Declaration on Environment and Development while reaffirming the principles adopted at Stockholm also asserted the need for sustainable development. The Rio Declaration proclaims that," Human beings are at the center of concerns for sustainable development. Human beings are entitled to a healthy and productive life in harmony with nature." (*Report of the United Nations Conference on Environment and Development Rio de Janeiro, 3-14 June 1992 A/CONF.151/26/Rev.1 (Vol. 1)* , n.d.) Every country should devise its developmental policies cognizant of its responsibilities towards the environment. All human beings share equal rights over natural resources and are also equally responsible for protecting them. We should ensure proper and mindful use of resources to achieve economical as well as social development without undermining the urgent need to prevent environmental degradation.

During the 2002 World Summit on Sustainable Development held in Johannesburg, South Africa, the world community reaffirmed their commitment to sustainable development. Johannesburg Declaration on Sustainable Development stated that, "Peace, security, stability and respect for human rights and fundamental freedoms including the right to development as well as respect for cultural diversity are essential for achieving sustainable development and ensuring that sustainable development benefits all." (*Report of the World Summit on Sustainable Development Johannesburg, South Africa*, n.d.) Recently, UNGA passed a resolution on 28 July 2022 recognizing the basic human right to a clean, healthy and sustainable environment. (*In Historic Move, UN Declares Healthy Environment a Human Right*, n.d.) Since the Stockholm Declaration in 1972, United Nations has played a major role in prompting countries to recognize the right to a healthy environment as a fundamental right in their national constitutions, to enact laws to protect the environment and related human rights and to devise policies to ensure development with sustainability.

Constitutional Recognition at the International Level :

Governments should ensure that people have access to all the information related to their environment and should also conduct campaigns and programs to create awareness about environmental problems and their rights related to the environment. Public awareness about environmental rights is a necessary step towards solving environmental issues as it fixes the accountability of governments and makes them responsible for protecting people's life and property from harm caused by environmental degradation. This way the public can also become a part of the decision-making process related to environmental issues.

Constitutional recognition of the right to a healthy environment enables the citizens of a country to actively participate in the enactment of environmental laws and ensure protection of the environment. Although almost every country has laws designed to check pollution levels, conserve its flora and fauna and other natural resources but still private companies and bureaucrats can violate such laws. The government agencies responsible for their proper enforcement often act weak and corrupt, making the implementation of such laws difficult. In such a scenario, vulnerable and poor sections of society struggle to save their environment from the harmful activities of corporates and governments. When the right to a healthy environment is recognized by a nation's constitution, it allows the citizens to raise voice against the implementation of such developmental policies that violate their fundamental right. Environmental rights may act as a powerful catalyst in the movement to save our environment as these empower the ordinary people of a nation to unite and fight for their right to live in a non-toxic and healthy environment.

As of 2017, more than 100 countries have recognized the right to a healthy environment in their constitutions. Countries such as Algeria, Argentina, Belgium, Brazil, Chile, France, Indonesia, Iraq, Kenya, Norway, Philippines, Russia, Spain, Turkey and Ukraine have constitutionally protected the right to a healthy environment whereas Australia, Bangladesh, China, Germany, India, Iran, Poland, Sri Lanka and Sweden have made constitutional provisions for a healthy environment. (*What Are Your Environmental Rights?* | *UNEP - UN Environment Programme*, n.d.) Other countries have also started making efforts to constitutionally recognize environmental rights and make provisions to protect them like any other fundamental right. Several U.S. states like Washington, New Jersey, New Mexico, Maryland, Oregon and Vermont have made efforts to constitutionalize environmental rights through amendments at their levels. (*New York Becomes the Third State to Adopt a Constitutional Green Amendment*, n.d.) On November 2, 2021, the state of New York passed an amendment to its state constitution that will give every citizen of New York the right to clean air and water and a healthful environment. (*Environmental Rights Amendment Passes in New York* | *Earthjustice*, n.d.) But still some countries like the UK are yet to incorporate the right to a healthy environment into their constitutions. (*Why Recognition of the Human Right to a Healthy Environment Is Essential – Inside Track*, n.d.) After the historical declaration by UNGA of recognizing a clean, healthy and sustainable environment as a human right, it becomes the responsibility of individual states to recognize this right constitutionally and ensure its implementation through legal protection.

The Indian Scenario :

The Constitution of India has made specific provisions for environmental protection by enacting various acts such as Wildlife (Protection) Act, 1972, Forest (Conservation) Act, 1980, Water (Prevention and Control of Pollution) Act, 1974, Air (Prevention and Control of Pollution) Act, 1981 and Environment Protection Act, 1986. Although the right to a healthy environment is not incorporated in the constitution as a basic human right but the fundamental rights recognized in the constitution indirectly affirm the existence of this right which at times has also been stated in the various judgements passed by the judiciary of India. The part III of the Indian Constitution deals with the fundamental rights (Articles 12-35). These are the basic human rights guaranteed and protected by the Constitution of India. Every citizen of this country is entitled to these rights by birth alone.

Article 21 of the Constitution says, "No person shall be deprived of his life or personal liberty except according to procedure established by law." Article 21 recognizes the right to life as a basic human right. The meaning of 'Life' in this article has been defined by courts from time to time. In Kharak Singh v. State of Uttar Pradesh AIR 1963 SC 1295, the Hon'ble Supreme Court of India said that the term 'Life' is something more than mere animal existence. (*Article 21 of Indian Constitution- Right to Life and Personal Liberty*, n.d.) In the case of Rural Litigation and Entitlement Kendra vs. State, AIR 1988 SC 2187 (popularly known as Dehradun Quarrying Case), it was recognized that the right to live in a healthy environment is a part of Article 21 of the Constitution. (*Environment Protection under Constitutional Framework of India*, n.d.)

In M.C. Mehta vs. Union of India AIR 1987 SC 1086, the right to live in a pollution free environment was also recognized as a part of the right to life in Article 21 of the Constitution. (*Constitution of India and Environmental Law - LawPage*, n.d.) Indian Constitution besides providing provisions to recognize the right to a healthy and safe environment as a fundamental right also expects its citizens to perform their fundamental duty of protecting the environment. Part-IV A of the Constitution deals with fundamental duties which are listed under Article 51-A. Article 51-A(g) states that," It shall be the duty of every citizen of India to protect and improve the natural environment including forests, lakes, rivers and wildlife and to have compassion for living creatures.". (*Article 51A(g) in The Constitution Of India 1949*, n.d.) The rights pertaining to a healthy environment play a significant role in environmental protection. But it is equally essential that we uphold our duties to preserve and safeguard the environment.

Conclusion and Suggestions :

It is evident that environmental protection and human rights are intertwined. A safe and healthy environment is necessary for the full enjoyment of human rights and to guarantee that our environment stays safe and healthy, it is crucial to assert that it is a fundamental human right. By declaring the right to a clean, healthy and sustainable environment as a basic human right, the United Nations has made the most significant step. Now is the time for all nations to constitutionally recognize environmental rights and frame laws that guarantee their protection, as only then can we hope to halt the widespread environmental devastation. Every individual on this planet, regardless of his nationality, has an equal right to the environment, thus we must view it as a shared global resource. However rich people have long adopted an unsustainable approach in using natural resources resulting in their rapid depletion and leading to environmental problems. Now the poor and weaker sections of society bear the brunt of their actions. The human rights approach in this situation can serve as a solution, only if the state recognizes these rights and establishes local bodies that may step in when those rights are violated. Making legislation that link environmental protection to human rights is a crucial step because it gives the common man authority over the wealthy and powerful. India, in particular, must move in this direction because environmental deterioration is a pressing problem in this country.

References :
Article 21 of Indian Constitution- Right to Life and Personal Liberty. (n.d.). Retrieved January 26, 2023, from https://legalstudymaterial.com/article-21-right-to-life-and-personal-liberty/

Article 51A(g) in The Constitution Of India 1949. (n.d.). Retrieved January 29, 2023, from https://indiankanoon.org/doc/1644544/

Climate Explainer: Climate Change and Air Pollution. (n.d.). Retrieved January 29, 2023, from https://www.worldbank.org/en/news/feature/2022/09/01/what-you-need-to-know-about-climate-change-and-air-pollution

Constitution of India and Environmental Law - LawPage. (n.d.). Retrieved January 26, 2023, from https://lawpage.in/environment/constitution-and-environment

Environment Protection under Constitutional Framework of India. (n.d.). Retrieved January 26, 2023, from https://pib.gov.in/newsite/printrelease.aspx?relid=105411

Environmental Rights Amendment Passes in New York | Earthjustice. (n.d.). Retrieved January 29, 2023, from https://earthjustice.org/news/press/2021/environmental-rights-amendment-passes-in-new-york

Fuller, R., Landrigan, P. J., Balakrishnan, K., Bathan, G., Bose-O'Reilly, S., Brauer, M., Caravanos, J., Chiles, T., Cohen, A., Corra, L., Cropper, M., Ferraro, G., Hanna, J., Hanrahan, D., Hu, H., Hunter, D., Janata, G., Kupka, R., Lanphear, B., … Yan, C. (2022). Pollution and health: a progress update. The Lancet Planetary Health, 6(6), e535–e547. https://doi.org/10.1016/S2542-5196(22)00090-0

In historic move, UN declares healthy environment a human right. (n.d.). Retrieved January 27, 2023, from https://www.unep.org/news-and-stories/story/historic-move-un-declares-healthy-environment-human-right

Khan, I., Hou, F., & Le, H. P. (2021). The impact of natural resources, energy consumption, and population growth on environmental quality: Fresh evidence from the United States of America. Science of The Total Environment, 754, 142222. https://doi.org/10.1016/J.SCITOTENV.2020.142222

New York Becomes the Third State to Adopt a Constitutional Green Amendment. (n.d.). Retrieved January 29, 2023, from https://www.bdlaw.com/publications/new-york-becomes-the-third-state-to-adopt-a-constitutional-green-amendment/

Report of the United Nations Conference on Environment and Development Rio de Janeiro, 3-14 June 1992 A/CONF.151/26/Rev.l (Vol. l) . (n.d.).

Report of The United Nations Conference on The Human Environment. Stockholm 5-16 June,1972. A/CONF./48/14/Rev.1. (n.d.).

Report of the World Summit on Sustainable Development Johannesburg, South Africa. (n.d.).

What are your environmental rights? | UNEP - UN Environment Programme. (n.d.). Retrieved January 28, 2023, from https://www.unep.org/explore-topics/environmental-rights-and-governance/what-we-do/advancing-environmental-rights/what-0

Why recognition of the human right to a healthy environment is essential – Inside track. (n.d.). Retrieved January 28, 2023, from https://greenallianceblog.org.uk/2022/09/15/why-recognition-of-the-human-right-to-a-healthy-environment-is-essential/

World Bank Group, T. (2022). The Global Health Cost of PM2.5 Air Pollution. The Global Health Cost of PM2.5 Air Pollution: A Case for Action Beyond 2021. https://doi.org/10.1596/978-1-4648-1816-5

Zhu, Y. G., Ioannidis, J. P. A., Li, H., Jones, K. C., & Martin, F. L. (2011). Understanding and harnessing the health effects of rapid urbanization in China. Environmental Science and Technology, 45(12), 5099–5104. https://doi.org/10.1021/ES2004254/ASSET/IMAGES/LARGE/ES-2011-004254_0002.JPEG

Assistant Professor
M.S.J Govt. P.G. College
Bharatpur (Rajasthan)
email : deepikasingh081720@gmail.com

10. Role of Ethics in Creating a Sustainable Future

Akash Sadanand Naik Salgaonkar

Abstract

Contemporary thinkers, philosophers, politicians and leaders give immense significance to sustainability, and for a good reason. Mother Earth faces numerous environmental challenges, including climate change, pollution, and resource depletion, because of a particular species: humans. To address these issues, we need to create a sustainable future that balances economic, social, and environmental factors. However, achieving sustainability is more than just a matter of implementing political policies and the latest technologies and focusing on the goals of humans. It requires a fundamental shift in our core values and behaviours with the component of Ethics. It is necessary to switch from an anthropocentric to Eco-centric philosophy and bring it to reality. This is where ethics comes in. Ethics provides a framework for making decisions that are not only good for humans but also good for every species all over the planet. This research paper explores the role of ethics in creating a sustainable future. The discussion of how basic ethical principles, such as responsibility, accountability, and respect for nature, can guide every individual towards more sustainable practices concerning nature is an essential part of this paper. The paper will also examine the importance of ethical leadership and ethical consumerism in driving sustainable development. Ultimately, the goal is to argue that ethics is not just a nice-to-have but a necessary component for achieving a sustainable future.

In the contemporary world, achieving sustainable development and protecting the environment has become pressing concern. Ethics stands out as valid among the multiple solutions proposed by various thinkers and philosophers to address this issue. Ethics studies moral principles and values that guide human behaviour to excellence. By adopting ethical principles and values, creating a sustainable future for all beings and future generations of human beings is possible. This research paper will explore the role of ethics in achieving sustainable development while protecting the environment. It discusses how ethical principles such as responsibility, accountability, and respect for nature can guide our actions towards a sustainable future. The paper will also examine how unethical practices such as pollution, deforestation, and overconsumption have contributed to environmental degradation and diminished sustainable development growth.

Furthermore, the paper will highlight the importance of ethical leadership in promoting sustainable development. Leaders who prioritise ethical principles and values can inspire their followers to adopt sustainable practices and create a culture of sustainability. The paper will also discuss how ethical consumerism can drive sustainable development by encouraging individuals to make environmentally conscious choices. The paper argues that ethics is the only solution for achieving sustainable development and protecting the environment. By adopting ethical principles and values, the creation of a sustainable future for future generations is possible.

The world faces several environmental challenges, including climate change, pollution, and resource depletion. Creating a sustainable future that balances economic, social, and environmental factors is necessary to address these issues. However, achieving sustainability is more than just implementing policies and technologies. It also requires a fundamental shift in our values and behaviours. That is where ethics comes in. Ethics provides a framework for making good decisions for humans and the planet.

What is Sustainability?
Sustainability is the extraordinary ability to meet the needs of the present generations of all species without reducing the possibility and ability of future generations to meet their own needs. It is a concept that encompasses economic, social, and environmental factors. To achieve sustainability, we must balance these three factors to ensure we are not depleting our resources or harming the environment. *Sustainable development* is a concept that has gained much attention in recent years. It refers to the necessary

development that meets the standards of sustainability in the present without compromising the standards of sustainability and the capability of future generations to meet their own needs. Sustainable development is essential to protect the environment, ensure social equity, and promote economic growth. However, achieving sustainable development is a challenging task. It requires a fundamental shift in our thinking about development and the environment. Ethics can be crucial in achieving sustainable development and protecting the environment. Ethics can be the only solution for achieving sustainable development and protecting the environment. Ethics in sustainability aims to change the way humans view and interact with nature. It requires a fundamental shift in our mindset from viewing nature as a resource to be exploited for the human benefit to recognising that we are a part of nature and that our well-being is deeply connected to the health of the natural world. For example, the issue of biodiversity and habitat loss is problematic even if they do not directly affect humans because every species has intrinsic value and plays a role in maintaining the balance of ecosystems. The tremendous loss of biodiversity can have cascading effects on the health of ecosystems, which can ultimately impact human well-being. Whether moral rights should be extended to nature is also a contentious issue. Some argue that nature has intrinsic value and should be protected for its own sake, while others argue that nature should be protected because it provides essential human services.

The obligation to protect future generations is another important ethical consideration in sustainability. One has a moral responsibility to ensure that one leaves the planet in a condition that is at least as good as inherited from the ancestors. This means mitigating climate change, protecting biodiversity, and ensuring that natural resources are used sustainably.

The Role of Ethics in Sustainability

Ethics provides a framework for making decisions that are not only good for humans but also good for the planet. Ethical principles such as responsibility, accountability, and respect for nature can guide us towards more sustainable practices. Ethics refers to the principles that govern human behaviour. It is a set of moral values that guide individuals and organisations in decision-making. Ethics is essential in achieving sustainable development because it provides a framework for decision-making that considers the long-term consequences of actions. Ethical decision-making considers the impact of actions on the environment, society, and future generations. Sustainable development requires balancing economic growth, social equity, and environmental protection. Ethics can help achieve this balance by guiding decision-makers to consider the impact of their actions on all three aspects of sustainable development. For example, ethical decision-making can help ensure that economic growth does not arrive at the expense of social equity or environmental protection. Ethics can also help address the root causes of unsustainable development. Unsustainable development is often the result of short-term thinking and a focus on immediate economic gains. Ethical decision-making can shift the focus to long-term sustainability and the well-being of future generations. By considering the long-term consequences of actions, ethical decision-making can help prevent unsustainable development.

Environmental protection is a critical aspect of sustainable development. The environment provides the resources that support economic growth and social well-being. However, human activities have significantly impacted the environment, leading to environmental degradation and climate change. Ethics can play a crucial role in protecting the environment by guiding decision-makers to consider the impact of their actions on the environment. Ethical decision-making can help prevent environmental degradation by promoting sustainable practices. For example, ethical decision-making can lead to adopting renewable, natural energy sources and reducing greenhouse gas emissions. Ethical decision-making can also promote the conservation of natural resources by encouraging responsible consumption and production practices.

Ethics can also help address environmental injustice. Environmental injustice focuses on the unequal distribution of environmental benefits and burdens. Ethical decision-making can ensure that environmental benefits and burdens are distributed fairly. For example, ethical decision-making can help prevent the siting of hazardous waste facilities in low-income communities. Ethics in sustainability refers to the moral principles and values that guide decision-making in sustainable development. It involves considering the impact of human actions on the natural world, other humans, and future generations. Ethical sustainability promotes fairness, justice, and equality in distributing resources and opportunities while protecting and conserving the natural environment. At the heart of ethics in sustainability is the recognition that humans are not the only beings that matter and that the welfare of non-human nature is also essential. This includes biodiversity, species health, and clean water and air availability. Failure to consider these factors during sustainable development can negatively impact humans and the natural world. While environmental ethics is a subset of ethics in sustainability, it focuses mainly on the relationship between human beings and nature and how specific aspects of nature can best be protected. Environmental ethics do not always consider sustainability's economic and social pillars simultaneously.

Environmental ethics is concerned with questions such as whether human beings have any moral authority to take, steal and use so much of the Earth's natural resources for their benefit, whether nature has its own set of values aside from its effects on human health and well-being, and whether human beings are necessarily superior to sentient beings, plant and animal species or other aspects of nature.

On the other hand, ethics in sustainability encompasses a broader range of ethical considerations beyond just the environment. It also includes social and economic considerations, such as equity, fairness, justice, equality, inclusiveness, and cultural differences. Ethics in sustainability requires decision-making processes that consider the needs of all stakeholders and are conducted in a socially just, environmentally responsible, and economically sustainable way.

Ethical sustainability requires making difficult choices that may not be the most convenient or profitable in the short term but are necessary for the greater good in the long term. This can involve investing more time and resources in sustainable practices and prioritising the needs of marginalised groups and future generations. Ethics in sustainability involves balancing the needs of humans and the natural world and making decisions that promote fairness, justice, and equality while protecting and conserving the environment for future generations. Ethical sustainability or Sustainability ethics does the practical switch from anthropocentric to eco-centric ethics. Ethics in sustainability is important because it provides a framework for decision-making that considers the long-term impact of our actions on the environment, society, and economy. Sustainability is about meeting the needs, not wants, of the present generations without truly compromising the capability of future generations to meet their own needs. Ethical considerations are essential to ensure that we are not sacrificing the well-being of future generations for our short-term gain.

Responsibility : Responsibility is the idea that we are accountable for our actions and their consequences. In sustainability, responsibility means we must take responsibility for our actions and their environmental impact. This includes reducing our carbon footprint, conserving resources, and minimising waste. One way to take responsibility for our actions is to adopt a circular economy model. This model is based on the idea of reducing waste and maximising the use of resources. It involves designing products and services that can be reused, repaired, or recycled. A circular economy model can reduce human environmental impact and create a more sustainable future.

Accountability : Accountability is the idea that we are responsible for the consequences of our actions. We must be accountable for our decisions and their environmental consequences in sustainability. This includes taking responsibility for our emissions, the waste every individual generate, and the resources we consume. One way to be accountable for our actions is to adopt a life cycle assessment approach. This approach involves assessing the environmental impact of a product or service throughout its entire life cycle, from production to disposal. By adopting a life cycle assessment approach, we can identify areas to reduce our environmental impact and create a more sustainable future.

Respect for Nature : Respect for nature is the idea that we should treat the environment with respect and dignity. In sustainability, respect for nature means protecting the environment and its resources. This includes conserving biodiversity, reducing pollution, and minimising our ecosystem impact. One way to show respect for nature is to adopt a sustainable agriculture model. This model involves using farming practices that are environmentally friendly and socially responsible. It involves using organic farming methods, conserving water, and reducing the use of pesticides and fertiliser use. We can protect the environment and create a more sustainable future by adopting a sustainable agriculture model.

The Importance of Ethical Leadership

Ethical leadership is the idea that leaders should act in a way that is ethical and responsible. In sustainability, ethical leadership means leaders should be responsible for their organisation's environmental impact. This includes reducing emissions, conserving resources, and minimising waste. One way to demonstrate ethical leadership is to adopt a sustainability strategy. This strategy should be based on responsibility, accountability, and respect for nature. It should involve setting goals and targets for reducing emissions, conserving resources, and minimising waste. By adopting a sustainability strategy, leaders can demonstrate their commitment to creating a more sustainable future. Another important ethical principle in sustainability is the idea of distributive justice. This principle recognises that the benefits and burdens of sustainability must be shared fairly among all members of society. We must ensure everyone can access clean air, water, food, and other basic needs. Everyone here includes all living beings, animals, plants, and all sentient being considered. It also means that we must consider the needs of vulnerable populations, such as low-income communities, indigenous peoples, endangered species, injured animals and beings bred in captivity who may be disproportionately affected by environmental degradation.

The Importance of Ethical Consumerism

Ethical consumerism is the idea that consumers should make purchasing decisions that are ethical and responsible. In the context of sustainability, ethical consumerism means that consumers should choose products and services that are environmentally friendly and socially responsible. This includes choosing products made from sustainable materials that are produced using environmentally friendly methods and packaged in an environmentally friendly way. One way to practice ethical consumerism is to look for eco-labels. Eco-labels indicate that a product or service has been produced using environmentally friendly methods. By choosing products and services that have eco-labels, consumers can support environmenttally friendly practices and create a more sustainable future. These are small and simple things everyone can follow in their everyday life. The relationship between ecosystem health and human needs is also complex. While humans have legitimate needs that must be met, these needs should not come at the expense of the health of ecosystems. Instead, we should strive to find ways to meet our needs in ethics, which can be applied to the three pillars of sustainability: environmental, social, and economic. Ethics play a crucial role in sustainability, as they provide an ethical foundation for decision-making processes that consider equity, fairness, justice, equality, inclusiveness, and cultural differences.

The Role of Ethics in Social Equity

Social equity is another critical aspect of sustainable development. Social equity refers to the fair distribution of resources and opportunities. Sustainable development requires social equity because it is essential to ensure that all individuals have complete access to all the resources and every opportunity needed to thrive. Ethics can play a crucial role in promoting social equity by guiding decision-makers to consider the impact of their actions on disadvantaged communities. Ethical decision-making can help promote social equity by addressing the root causes of inequality. For example, ethical decision-making can lead to policies promoting equal access to education and healthcare. Ethical decision-making can also promote fair labour practices by ensuring workers are paid a living wage and have safe working conditions. One of the fundamental ethical principles in sustainability is the concept of intergenerational equity. This principle recognises that we have a moral obligation to leave the planet in a condition that is at least as good as the one we inherited from our ancestors. This means we must use natural resources sustainably so that future generations can benefit from them. It also means that we need to consider the long-term impact of our actions on nature and the environment and take essential steps to mitigate any adverse effects. Social ethics in sustainability targets the actions, attitudes, beliefs, cultural traditions, and decisions an individual makes. It provides a fundamental ethical foundation on which any group can make sustainable decisions in a way that considers the social costs, benefits, and values of a decision. Economic ethics are closely related to social ethics, as many ethical, economic decisions are based on the heavy social consequences or costs associated with that economic activity or decision. Economic ethics consider a product's efficiency, productivity, and security and whether it has been produced in an environment that provides fair wages and working conditions. Environmental ethics can be the crucial element that helps social ethics evolve. Environmental ethics focuses on everything beyond humans, the value of non-human nature and the living and non-living qualities within nature. It considers what actions are right and wrong in natural environments and focuses on preserving biodiversity, clean water and air, and the value of non-human life. Environmental ethics argue that humans are responsible for coexisting with non-human nature and protecting it for future generations.

The Role of Ethics in Economic Growth

Economic growth is critical to sustainable development. Economic growth provides the resources needed to support social well-being and environmental protection. Economic growth can lead to sustainable development if social equity and environmental protection are balanced. Ethics can play a crucial role in promoting sustainable economic growth by guiding decision-makers to consider the impact of their actions on all three aspects of sustainable development. Ethical decision-making can help promote sustainable economic growth by encouraging responsible business practices. For example, ethical decision-making can lead to adopting sustainable production practices that reduce waste and promote resource efficiency. Ethical decision-making can also promote fair trade practices that ensure workers are paid a fair wage and have safe working conditions. In addition to these ethical principles, sustainability requires a holistic approach that considers the interconnectedness of environmental, social, and economic systems. This means that we all can be economically stable and help the unfit to survive.

Conclusion

The role of ethics in creating a sustainable future cannot be overstated. Ethics play a crucial role in sustainability, as it ensures that decision-making processes consider the needs of all stakeholders and are conducted in a socially just, environmentally responsible, and economically sustainable way. Integrating ethics into sustainability practices can create a more just and sustainable world. Ethics provides a framework for making decisions that are not only good for us but also good for the planet. The principles of responsibility, accountability, and respect for nature can guide us towards more sustainable practices. Ethical leadership and ethical consumerism are also crucial in driving sustainable development. Creating a sustainable future requires a fundamental shift in our values and behaviours. By adopting ethical principles and practices, we can create a more sustainable future for ourselves and future generations. We must take responsibility for our actions and make choices that support a sustainable future. Together, one can create a world that is not only prosperous but also environmentally friendly and socially responsible. Ethics can be the only solution for achieving sustainable development and protecting the environment. The study suggests that explicitly making the nuances and presuppositions that underlie various versions of the anti-anthropocentric rhetoric is necessary to foster constructive dialogue among different anti-anthropocentrism proponents and their detractors. This approach can help to identify common ground and facilitate the development of practical solutions to the environmental crisis.

The paper also suggests that while environmental ethics is an essential aspect of ethics in sustainability, more is needed on its own. To achieve sustainability, decision-making processes must consider all three pillars of sustainability: environmental, social, and economical, and must be conducted in an ethical manner that considers the needs of all stakeholders.

This article presents a comprehensive analysis of anthropocentrism being the cause of the global environmental crisis. The study drew on multiple perspectives of ethics and extended the boundaries of ethics to include all living things. Understanding sustainability ethics provides a nuanced understanding of the various usages of the term 'anthropocentrism' and the underlying disagreements among proponents of anti-anthropocentrism. The article argues that while anthropocentric actions have been identified as the root of the environmental crisis, and tries to bring a new ethical scope to address the complex interplay of factors contributing to the crisis. The study identifies the human-nature dichotomy, capitalism, unethical consumerism, and industrialism as underlying assumptions and views that ethics attached to sustainability work together to protect the environment. The article also highlights environmentalists' challenges in their attempts to go beyond anthropocentrism: but now ethics is the only solution. This research paper challenges previous anthropocentric ethical notions and emphasises eco-centric ethics and the need for a more nuanced and comprehensive approach to addressing the environmental crisis.

In conclusion, this article contributes to the ongoing debate on the relationship between ethics and sustainability, anthropocentrism and ecocentrism, the global environmental crisis and its possible ethical solutions. By highlighting the ability of ethics to resolve the environmental crisis, the study emphasises the need for a more comprehensive and nuanced approach to addressing the complex interplay of factors contributing to the crisis.

References :
Becker, C. (2011). *Sustainability Ethics and Sustainability Research*. Springer Netherlands.
Boylan, M. (2020). *Basic Ethics*. Routledge, Taylor and Francis Group.

Boylan, M. (Ed.). (2022). *Environmental Ethics*. Wiley.

Charles, R. (Ed.). (2016). *Environmental Ethics and Sustainability*. Callisto Reference.

Curry, P. (2011). *Ecological Ethics: An Introduction*. Wiley.

Düwell, M., Bos, G., & Steenbergen, N. v. (Eds.). (2018). *Towards the Ethics of a Green Future: The Theory and Practice of Human Rights for Future People*. Taylor & Francis.

Ip, K.-T. (Ed.). (2009). *Environmental Ethics: Intercultural Perspectives*. Rodopi.

Keller, D. R. (Ed.). (2010). *Environmental Ethics: The Big Questions*. Wiley.

Meinhold, R. (2021). *Business Ethics and Sustainability*. Taylor & Francis.

Newton, L. H. (2003). *Ethics and Sustainability: Sustainable Development and the Moral Life*. Prentice Hall.

Russ, J. (2018). *Sustainability and Design Ethics, Second Edition*. CRC Press.

Ryan, M. (2016). *Human Value, Environmental Ethics and Sustainability: The Precautionary Ecosystem Health Principle*. Rowman & Littlefield International.

Taback, H., & Ramanan, R. (2013). *Environmental Ethics and Sustainability: A Casebook for Environmental Professionals*. CRC Press.

Tharakan, K. (2011). Anthropocentrism and Ecocentrism: on the Metaphysical Debate in Environmental Ethics. *Jadavpur Journal of Philosophy*, *21*, 27-42.

Thiele, L. P., Monroe, M. C., Peterson, A. L., Kibert, C. J., & Plate, R. R. (2011). *Working Toward Sustainability: Ethical Decision-Making in a Technological World*. Wiley.

PhD Research Scholar
School of Sanskrit, Philosophy, and Indic Studies,
Goa University. Taligao, Goa, 403206.
email : **akash6459@gmail.com**

11. Review of the Recent Advances and Applications of Laser-induced Breakdown Spectroscopy (LIBS) in Environmental Monitoring

V. Shyamala Devi[*]

Abstract

The analysis of geological and environmental materials is the current and growing requirement in the recent years. LIBS (Laser-Induced Breakdown Spectroscopy) is a spectroscopic technique based on atomic emission and has been used as an analysis tool of minerals, rocks, soils, sediments etc. LIBS has the advantage of faster analysis than other techniques with a typical detection limits of elements. Applications of laser-induced breakdown spectroscopy (LIBS) have been growing rapidly and continue to be extended to a broad range of materials. The paper presents the applications of LIBS exclusively for the analysis of environmental materials. However, before discussing the reviews on LIBS applications on environmental monitoring; a brief overview of the fundamental of the LIBS analytical technique, double-pulse and femtosecond LIBS methods, its instrumentation, sampling techniques and analysis of minerals, rocks, soils, sediments and other natural materials are presented. LIBS technology is the increasing requirement for the quality control in the environment due to the various pollutants. The review focuses on the most relevant advances and is reported in different sections relative to the analyzed objects.

Keywords : Nd-YAG Laser, Laser-Induced Breakdown Spectroscopy (LIBS), Plasma, environmental monitoring

1. Introduction

The applications of laser-induced breakdown spectroscopy (LIBS) have been widely studied in versatile fields such as environmental monitoring[1-4], biomedical applications[5], mars[6,7] and space exploration[8]. Laser induced breakdown spectroscopy (LIBS) is a form of optical excitation in which the sample is vaporized by a high energy laser pulse and forms a luminous plasma. The light from the plasma is temporally resolved (to discriminate against the continuum emission from the plasma) and wavelength dispersed to obtain information regarding the composition of the material that was laser vaporized. This technique has received considerable attention in recent years as a versatile analytical technique, particularly in environmental applications, as it offers several advantages: a) small sample size required for analysis, b) direct analysis of inhomogenous materials (without the need for any sample preparation), and c) small turnaround time between sample submission and analysis. All the above advantages become particularly attractive in the analysis of environmental samples. In this method, the sample is first vaporized by a focused, high energy laser pulse. Usually the fundamental (1064 nm) or the second harmonic (532 nm) of a YAG laser, with pulse energies in the realm of 20 to 50 mJ/pulse is used. Emission from the laser plasma is sampled through a collection lens and focused onto a spectrometer. As emission in the first ~100 ns after the laser pulse, is dominated by the continuum emission from the plasma, the detection must be delayed, for this light to decay. The latter part of the emission is dominated by emission from the elements of interest in the analyte sample, which must be selectively detected. The detection system of the spectrometer must therefore be equipped to gate the observation suitably. Further, for the detection system to have multielement capabilities, an array type detector, such as a CCD array is necessary (instead of a single channel photomultiplier). The elemental composition determined by the wet chemical analysis process has major limitations such as the detection limit, time consuming, and does not provide an immediate feed-back to the environmentalist. The environmental monitoring groups thus to be supported by developing an on-line process for the estimation of elements. The elements that were estimated included transition metals, lanthanides, noble metals, p-block elements, with detection limits in the realm of 100 to 500 ppm. Any analytical method employed for the environmental monitoring must possess the following desirable characteristics: speed of analysis, on-line capability, amenable for remote operation, user-friendly, accuracy and precision. In addition to these characteristics, LIBS has also been used for the analysis of samples of any state such as solid[9], liquid[10] or gas[11].

2. Experimental
2.1. Experimental Set Up

Figure 1, shows the schematic of the experimental set up. It may be noted that the laser, lenses, beam steering optics, X-Y table for sample restoring and the multichannel spectrometer is required for the LIBS set-up.

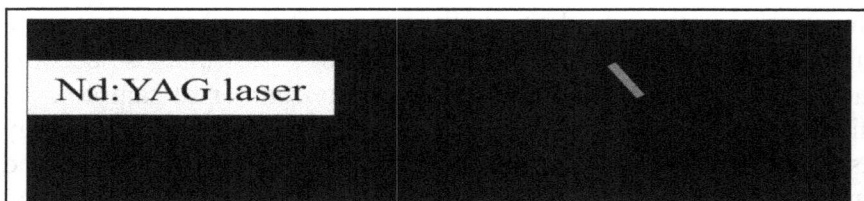

Figure 1: Schematic representation of a typical LIBS set-up.

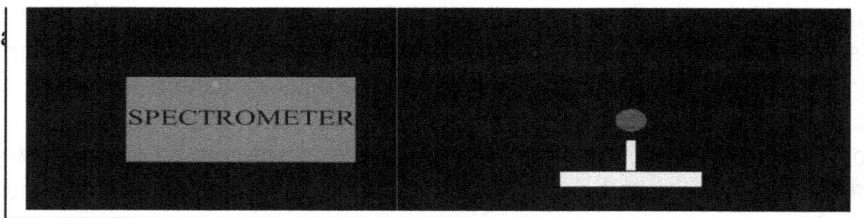

Figure 1: Schematic representation of a typical LIBS set-up.

2.2. Double-pulse LIBS and femtosecond LIBS

The double-pulse LIBS technique has been used for the analysis of synthetic glasses, rocks, steels [12]. The group have combined two Nd:YAG lasers emitting at 532 nm in the collinear beam geometry to carry out double-pulse experiments. The suitability of the double-pulse LIBS for different materials have been analysed based on the advantages and the limitations of the double-pulse laser-induced breakdown spectroscopy (LIBS) for analytical purpose. The trace level detection of carbon has been measured in standard steel samples using Single-pulse LIBS (SP-LIBS) and long-short double-pulse LIBS (LS-DP-LIBS) [13]. The quantitative analysis of carbon in steel samples has been achieved by, long-short double-pulse LIBS (LS-DP-LIBS) with pretreatment pulses. The quantitave analysis of Pb heavy metal in soil has been analysed using a femtosecondnanosecond double-pulsed laser-induced breakdown spectroscopy (fs-ns DP-LIBS) with a delay of 800 μs between the two lasers [14].

The femtosecond laser-induced breakdown spectroscopy (fs-LIBS) of Cu with the sample preheated to different temperatures (22–120 °C) has been reported Wang *etal* [15]. They have observed the dependence of the spectral intensity of the plasma emission with the target temperature and thus the enhanced the detection sensitivity of femtosecond LIBS. S.Zhao *etal* studied the femtosecond laser filamentation-induced breakdown spectroscopy (FIBS) combined with chemometrics methods for soil contamination monitoring application and thus improved the accuracy of heavy metal soil quantitative analysis [16]. The influence of femtosecond pulses in the analysis of solid samples such as brass, copper, aluminium and silicon (with different buffer gas and pressure) has been reported by Mateo *etal* [17]. The spectra recorded under air or argon atmosphere showed line broadening particularly at high ambient pressure.

3. Environmental Monitoring Applications Perceived with LIBS:

LIBS as a tool for environmental monitoring also finds wide application, in addition to industrial and nuclear applications [18], geological [19] and archaeological surveys [20] and defence applications [21]. L.F. Viana *etal.* used the LIBS technique for the detection of bioaccumulated Fe and Pb in scales of aquatic species, Salminus brasiliensis *and* Prochilodus lineatus; which showed the technique as a promising tool for environmental monitoring [22]. The analysis of impurity elements such as molybdenum (Mo), tungsten (W), carbon (C), copper (Cu), lithium (Li), titanium (Ti), silicon (Si), iron (Fe), and chromium (Cr) deposited on the test tiles was studied [23]. LIBS has showed effective in the depth-resolved identification of impurities deposited on the tiles. The analysis of solid fertilizer samples for the different contaminants (Cd, Cr and Pb) and other micronutrient elements (B, Cu, Mn, Zn, Ca and Mg) has been studied using LIBS [24]. One of the major applications studied with this equipment is the evaluation of elemental composition such as minerals and metal on vegetal tissues [25].

While remote online analysis can be estimated using pulsed excimer laser ArF, fibre optics and a high resolution spectrometer, univariate and multivariate analysis exist for in depth information from the LIBS experiment. Hence this technique is attractive as it has the potential to be adapted for a remote, on-line measurement. In addition to the above major application, there are various other applications related to the industries that have been described in the literature, some of which are mentioned below.

S.Trautner *etal.* demonstrated the vulcanizing system of rubber can be quantified under ambient conditions with LIBS and the technique as process analytical sensor by itself [26]. Another application of interest to industries is the measurement of coal composition through the analysis of spectral features corresponding to the various classifications of coals[27]. LIBS has been used for the analysis of trace heavy metals in soils [28]. LIBS-assisted by laser-induced fluorescence (LIBS-LIF) was utilized for the selective enhancement effect of spectral intensities of the interfered lines. Likewise, estimation of Pb in soils has been reported with detection limits in the range of 0.6 ppm. LIBS has also been employed for the analysis of elemental composition changes in battery electrode materials to establish the quantitative elemental ratios of Ni, Mn, Co and trace transition metals, Cr, Mo in cathode material samples, allowing, therefore, for process control and quality assurance of the battery electrode materials involved in automotive and various electronic devices [29]. Analysis of proteins in wheat flour and whole meal samples melts has also been achieved using LIBS, which has application as a quality parameter in terms of price, nutritional value and labelling in industries [30]. LIBS has also been used for monitoring elements in waste printed circuit boards (PCB) as recycling source [31]. The elements that were estimated, included Al and Pb and the sample analyzed contain Al in the realm of 3 and 55 g Kg^{-1}. Isotopic analysis of Li and U were estimated by LIBS and laser ablation-tuneable diode laser absorption spectroscopy (LA-TDLAS) [32]. For example, $^{235}U/^{238}U$ ratios have been measured using this method and thus the possibility of rapid elemental and isotopic analysis across the nuclear fuel cycle. A portable LIBS spectrometer is also available for field analysis [33].

4. Conclusion

The detection of elements at trace level has been reported in various works. The major highlight of the review is the observation of spectral lines of elements by suitably tailoring the ambient conditions such as spectral interferences using time delayed detection, thus serving as an environmental monitoring tool. The result on the effect of hybrid LIBS such as LA-TDLAS, LIBS-LIF on the spectral measurements have greatly aided in extending the applications of environmental monitoring. This review reports the use of LIBS for the application of the technique in environmental monitoring.

Acknowledgement

The author would like to acknowledge fruitful discussions with research scholars from the research group of the Radiochemistry Laboratory, Indira Gandhi Centre for Atomic Research, Kalpakkam, Tamil Nadu.

References

1. R. Yi, X. Yang, R. Zhou, J. Li, H. Yu, Z. Hao, L. Guo, X. Li, Y. Lu, X. Zeng, *Anal. Chem.*, 2018 90 (11) 7080.
2. R.A. Multari, D.A. Cremers, T. Scott, P. Kendrick, *J.Agr. & Food Chem.*, 2013 61 (10) 2348.
3. M.A. Gondal, M.N. Siddiqui, M.M. Nasr, *Energy Fuels*, 2010 24 (2) 1099.
4. A. Harhira, J. El Haddad, A. Blouin, M. Sabsabi, *Energy & Fuels*, 2018 32 (3) 3189.
5. T. Kim, Z.G. Specht, P.S. Vary, C. T. Lin, *The J.Phys.Chem.B*, 2004 108 (17) 5477.
6. C. Alvarez-Llamas, P. Purohit, J. Moros, J. Laserna, *Anal. Chem.*, 2022 94 (3) 1840.
7. J. Moros, M.M. ElFaham & J.J. Laserna, Anal. Chem., 2018 90 (3), 2079.
8. D.A. Cremers, 'Remote Analysis by LIBS: Application to Space Exploration' Applied Research Associates, Inc., 2008, USA.

9. R. Pamu, S. Ali Davari, D. Darbar, E.C. Self, J. Nanda, D. Mukherjee *ACS Appl. Ener. Mater.,* 2021 *4* (7), 7259.

10. E.M. Cahoon & J.R. Almirall, *Anal. Chem.,* 2012 (84), 5, 2239.

11. Tian-Jia Jiang, M. Yang, Shan-Shan Li, Ming-Jun Ma, Nan-Jing Zhao, Z. Guo, Jin-Huai Liu, and Xing-Jiu Huang, *Anal. Chem.,* 2017 89 (10) 5557.

12. C. Gautier, P. Fichet, D. Menut, J. Dubessy, *Spectrochim. Acta B: Atomic Spectroscopy,* 2006 61(2) 210.

13. M. Cui, H. Guo, Y. Chi, L. Tan, C. Yao, D. Zhang, Y. Deguchi, *Spectrochim. Acta B: Atomic Spectroscopy,* 2022 191 106398.

14. S. Zhao, C. Song, X. Gao, *Results in Physics,* 2019, 15, 102736.

15. Q. Wang, A. Chen, H. Qi, S. Li, Y. Jiang, M. Jin, *Optics & Laser Technology,* 2020, 121, 105773.

16. S. Zhao, M. Sher Afghan, H. Zhu, X. Gao, *Optik,* 2022, 251, 168444.

17. M.P. Mateo, V. Piñon, D. Anglos, G. Nicolas, *Spectrochim. Acta B: Atomic Spectroscopy,* 2012, 74-75, 18.

18. P. Coffey, N. Smith, B. Lennox, G. Kijne, B. Bowen, A. Davis-Johnston, P.A. Martin, *J. of Hazardous Materials,* 2021, 412, 125193.

19. S.N.P.panya, A.H. Galmed, M. Maaza, B.M. Mothudi, M.A. Hari th, *Materials today: Proceedings,* 2021, 36(2), 600.

20. *K. Melessanaki, M. Mateo, S.C. Ferrence, P.P. Betancourt, D. Anglos,* Appl. Surf. Science, *2002, 197-198, 156.*

21. J.L. Gottfried, Laser-Induced Breakdown Spectroscopy : Defense applications, Second Edition, 2020, 275.

22. L.F. Viana, Y.R. Súarez, C.A.L. Cardoso, S.M. Lima, L.Humberto da Cunha Andrade, S.E. Lima-Junior, 2019, 228, 258.

23. M. Imran, Z. Hu, F. Ding, M. Salman Khan, G.-N. Luo, A. Farooq, I. Ahmad, *Nuclear Materials and Energy,* 2023, 34, 101379.

24. D.F. Andrade and E.R. Pereira-Filho, *J. Agri.& Food Chem.,* 2016 64 (41), 7890.

25. M.R. Martelli, F. Brygo, A. Sadoudi, P. Delaporte, C. Barron, *J. Agri. & Food Chem.,* 2010 58 (12), 7126.

26. S. Trautner, J. Lackner, W. Spendelhofer, N. Huber, J.D. Pedarnig, *Anal. Chem.,* 2019 91 (8), 5200.
27. A. Metzinger, D. J. Palásti, É. Kovács-Széles, T. Ajtai, Z. Bozóki, Z. Kónya, G. Galbács, *Energy & Fuels*, 2016 30 (12), 10306.
28. R. Yi, J. Li, X. Yang, R. Zhou, H. Yu, Z. Hao, L. Guo, X. Li, X. Zeng, Y. Lu., Anal. Chem., 2017 89 (4), 2334.
29. R. Pamu, S. Ali Davari, D. Darbar, E.C. Self, J. Nanda, D. Mukherjee, *ACS Applied Energy Materials* 2021 4 (7), 7259.
30. B. Sezer, G. Bilge, I. H. Boyaci, *J. Agri. & Food Chem.,* 2016 *64* (49), 9459.
31. D.V. Babos, A.Cruz-Conesa, E.R. Pereira-Filho, J.M. Anzano, *Journal of Hazardous Materials*, 2020, 399, 122831.
32. G. Hull, E.D. McNaghten, C.A. Sharrad, P.A. Martin, *Spectrochim. Acta B: Atomic Spectroscopy*, 2022, 190, 106378.
33. G.S. Senesi, R.S. Harmon, R.R. Hark, *Spectrochim. Acta B: Atomic Spectroscopy*, 2021, 175, 106013.

*Department of Chemistry,
Dwaraka Doss Goverdhan Doss Vaishnav College (Autonomous)
(Affiliated to the University of Madras, Chennai),
Tamil Nadu, India

12. A Review on Green Synthesis of ZnO Nanoparticles using Leaf Extract and its Characterizations

Hajeera Aseen A[1,]
Jyolsna P[1],
Vivek P[2],
Parthasarathy M[1],
Gowthami V[1*]

Abstract

Nanoscience and nanotechnology deal with extremely small size of nanoparticles which ranges between 1 to 100 nm. The nanoparticles are used in many science fields such as physics, chemistry, biology, biomedicine, engineering and agricultural fields and so on. in medicine it plays a vital role in the world. It is very big advantages of nanotechnology. Different methods of synthesis of nanoparticles are divided into three types are listed here, physical method synthesis of nanoparticle, chemical method synthesis of nanoparticle and biological or green synthesis of nanoparticle. In physical and chemical method synthesis of nanoparticles are causes our environment. It causes harmful radiation, more toxic, pollutant, high cost and non-renewable energy resources that like many problems arrive. But in green synthesis method is environment friendly in nature. It is renewable energy, low cost. So, my article moves to green synthesis of nanoparticles and its applications.

Keywords : nanoparticles, green synthesis, applications.

1. Introduction

The new development in the field of science and technology, enormously nanotechnology has subsidized to the assorted submissions of metal oxide nanoparticles. Zinc oxide nanoparticles through high quality have been fictional effectively by engaging a green method using the leaf extract of the basil plant. The possessions of the changed calcination temperatures on the construction belongings such as morphology, shape, size, orientation, distribution, crystal structure quality, optical properties, and chemical arrangement of ZnO NPs have been deliberate in aspect.[1] Many procedures have been used to describe the biosynthesized ZnO NPs. green synthesized ZnO NPs in contradiction of the bacterial strains deliberate and therefore, they can be used as an operative antibacterial representative in industrial and pharmaceutical applications, such as food conserver packaging.[2] Newly, the biosynthesis of nanoparticles has been widely explored due to the wide variety of vital submissions in nanotechnology. Biosynthesized zinc oxide nanoparticles, ZnO NPs, have become increasingly important since they have many applications and are environmentally friendly.[3] The significance of this study is ZnO Nanoparticles has been synthesized through an easy method that avoids toxic chemicals and difficult experimental process.[4] According to Zeta potential analysis biosynthesis ZnO Nanoparticles in this study possess good stability. This result is good indicator that these Nano particles possess considerable active adsorption sites to absorb dyes, and heavy metal ions from aqueous system.[4] The photo catalytic degradation of ZnO Nanoparticles was estimated in reduction of methylene blue methylene by 54% and ZnO Nanoparticles can be used as photo catalytic for decomposition of organic pollution in present in water[5]. ZnO Nanoparticles reduced the band gap. In brief this is a simple, effective, biosynthetic method which could be an alternative for chemical and physical methods for the large scale production of ZnO Nanoparticles. The biosynthesized ZnO Nanoparticles from the difference leaf extract can be utilized for many application such as antibacterial[2,7,15,16,18,19,20,23to30], antioxidant[7], anti-inflammatory[7], ant diabetic[7], anticancer[7], anti microbial[14,17], antifungal [9] and photo catalytic activity.[2,5,7,14]

2. Green Synthesis

Traditional approaches are used from historical several years but investigates have verified that the green approaches are additional actual for the generation of NPs with the benefit of less balances of disappointment, little price and comfort of classification Physical and chemical tactics of manufacturing NPs have stood numerous pressures on environment due to their toxic metabolites. Plant-based synthesis of NPs is definitely not an upsetting way, a metal salt is synthesized through plant extract and the response is accomplished in proceedings to two some of times at representative room temperature. [8] Chemical and Physical methods have been consuming high radiation and extremely focused reducers and calming mediators that are injurious for the environmental and to human health. Hence, biological synthesis of nanoparticles is a solitary stage bio-reduction process and less energy is used to synthesize eco- friendly. [10] In over-all, green nano-biotechnology means synthesizing nanoparticles or the nonmaterial's using biological routes such as those connecting microorganisms, plants, and viruses or they're by products, such as proteins and lipids, with the help of various biotechnological tools.

Nanoparticles made by green technology are far superior to persons manufactured with physical and chemical methods created on various characteristics [11] .Typically, the green mode of nanoparticle synthesis is preferred over physical and chemical route of nanoparticle synthesis due to its inherent advantages such as use of non-toxic reagents, improved stability, informal scale-up, biocompatibility, sustainability, prompt and low energy requirements. Biological agents such as bacteria, fungi, yeasts and plants may be employed as bio-nano factories for eco-friendly-one-step-rapid synthesis of nanoparticles. These methods are being extensively studied because of their wide application in all areas of science[12] .The green synthesis of NPs using plant extracts has more advantages than using microorganisms. Because it is a single step method, is non-pathogenic and economic, produces a huge number of metabolites, is cost-effective, and is an eco-friendly approach [13]. Green synthesis of NPs aims at lessening waste generation and employing sustainable processes. Green chemistry synthesis routes are naturally friendly and non-hazardous, as well as cost operative. In the past, green processes using mild reaction conditions and nontoxic precursors have been accentuated in the development of nanotechnology for promoting environmental sustainability toward the production of NPs[14].

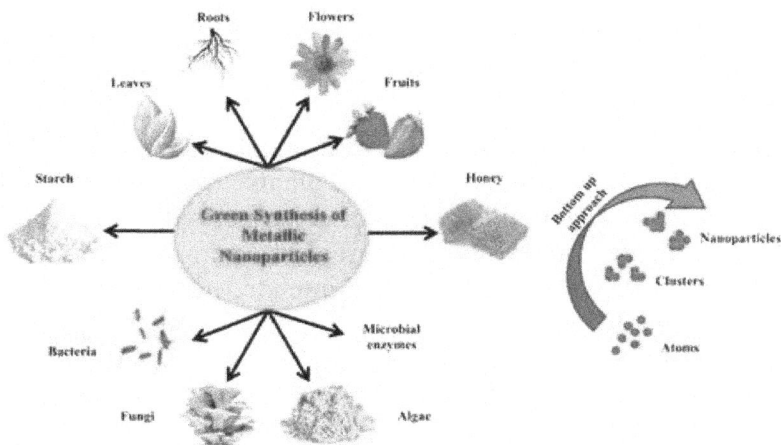

3. Extraction Methods

Extraction is the crucial first step in the analysis medicinal plants, because it is necessary to extract the desired chemical components from the material for further separation and characterizations. The purpose of all extractions is to separate the soluble plant metabolites leaving behind the insoluble cellular marc (residue). The initial crude extracts using these metabolites.

3.1. Choosing Extraction Methods

1. Stability to heat
2. Nature of the solvent
3. Cost of the drug
4. Duration of extraction
5. Final volume required
6. Intended use

3.2. Some Extraction Methods which used are discussed below

1. Maceration
2. Infusion
3. Percolation
4. Decoction
5. Digestion
6. Soxhlet extraction
7. Microwave assisted extraction
8. Ultrasound assisted extraction

9. Accelerated solvent extraction
10. Supercritical fluid extraction

3.2.1. Maceration

Maceration is a procedure use in wine manufacture and has been adopted and widely used in medical plants. Maceration involved soaking the plant material in a stopper container with a solvent. And it allowed standing room temperature for a period of minimum 3 days frequent agitation. The process intended to soften and break plant cell wall to release the soluble photochemical. After the 3 days, the mixture is pressed or strained by filtration. In this conventional method to heat transferred through convection and conduction.

3.2.2. Infusion

The infusion is carried out by immersing the plant parts to use in an amount of boiling water, allowed to stand 15 min and then filtered through a filter or filter paper. Infusion uses the same principle as maceration. Both are covered with cold water or boiled water. However, the maceration period for infusion is shorter and the sample is boiled in specified volume of water per a defined time for decoction.

3.2.3. Percolation

The percolator is a conical vessel with a top opening in which is placed a circular drilled lid allowing the pass liquid and subjecting the materials placed on in to a slight pressure. The bottom has a modifiable closure to allow opening of the fluid at a suitable rate. The plant material is moistened prior to their placement in the percolator with a proper amount of menstruum; it's placed in a sealed container and leave stand for approximately four hours. Later than that time the plant material should be suitably placed in the percolator so as to permit the still opening of fluid and the complete contact with the plant material. The percolator should be filled with liquid and enclosed up. The base outlet is opened until get a usual soaked and then closes. Extra menstruum is additional to envelop all the material and must place to immerse in the percolator stopped for 24 hours. After this time leave it to drip slowly and added enough menstruum to a proportional volume of 3/4 of the total volume for the fin al product. The soaked bunch is pushed to extract the greatest remaining fluid retained and supplemented with enough menstruum to get the appropriate proportion it is filtered or clarified by decantation. The process is usually done at moderate rate until the extraction is completed before evaporation to get a concentrated extracts.

3.2.4. Decoction

In this process the drug is boiled in water for 15 to 60 min it is cooled stained and added enough cold water through the drug to obtain the desired volume. Depending on the steadiness of the parts to extract, decoction times will be more or less extended; usually roots leaves, flowers and leafy stems are boiled in water for about 15 min, while the branches and other stiff parts can require up to an hour, through this time the evaporated water should be replacing. Once the decoction is done it is necessary to filter the liquid through a cloth, squeezing very well they obtained liquid. Does are similar to infusion ones, I-e. A plant part per ten of water, although for the plants with elevated mucilage contented in this case will be 1/20 to avoid the solution takes much viscosity. Decoction is mostly suitable for extracting heat- stable compounds, hard plants material and usually resulted in more oil -soluble compounds compared to maceration and infusion. The decoctions are arranged for using in the instant and shouldn't be stored for more than 24 hours.

3.2.5. Digestion

Digestion is a type of maceration with trivial warming during the extraction process, provided that the temperature does not alter the active ingredients of plant material and so there is superior efficiency in the use of menstruum. The most used temperatures are between 35°C and 40°C. , although can rise to no higher than 50°C. This process is used with the together plant parts or those that contain poorly soluble substances. We initiate the parts to extract in a container with the liquid pre-heated to the indicated temperatures, is maintained for a phased that may vary among half an hour and 24 hours, shaking the container regularly.

3.2.6. Soxhlet Extraction

In this method finely ground sample is placed in a porous bag or thimble made from a strong a strong filter paper or cellulose, which is place, is in thimble chamber of the soxhlet apparatus. Extraction solvents is heated in the base flask, vaporizes into the model thimble, condenses in the condenser and drip rear. When the liquid substance reaches the siphon arm, the liquid filling emptied into the bottom flask again and the procedure is sustained. This method requires a smaller quantity of solvent compared maceration. Though, the soxhlet extraction comes with difficulty such as experience to dangerous and flammable liquid organic solvents, with potential toxic emissions through extraction. Solvents used in the extraction system need to be high purity that might add to cost. This procedure is measured not environmental friendly and may give to pollution problem compared to go forward extraction method such as supercritical fluid extraction (SFE). The ideal sample for soxhlet extraction is also limited to dry and finely divided solid and may factors such as temperature, solvent-sample ratio and agitation speed need to be considered for this method.

3.2.7. Microwave Assisted Extraction (MAE)

MAE use microwave energy to make possible divider of analyses from the sample matrix into the solvent. Microwave radiation interacts with dipoles of polar and polarizable material causes heating near the surface of the material and heat transferred by conduction. Dipole rotation of the molecules provoked by microwave electromagnetic disrupts hydrogen bonding ornamental the migration of dissolved ions and promotes solvent diffusion into the matrix. In non polar solvents, unfortunate heating happen as the energy is transferred by dielectric absorption purely. Enhanced recoveries of analyzes and reproducibility were experimental in MAE method but with care of using good conditions to shun thermal degradation. Though this method is partial to small molecule phenolic compounds. Because these molecules were stable under microwave heating condition up to 100 °C for 20 min. In microwave assisted extraction (MAE), microwaves are used to heat the solvents in contact with the sample to extract the element preferred from the sample. In this method, we can divide the analyzes in just a small number of minutes, manufacture the procedure very effective and time-saving.

3.2.8. Ultrasound Assisted Extraction

20 kHz to 2000 KHZ ultrasound ranging involves the UAE. The mechanic effect of acoustics, cavitations from the ultrasound increase the surface contact between solvents and samples and permeability of cell walls. Physical and chemical properties of the materials subjected to ultrasound are altered and disrupt the plant cell wall facilitating release of compounds and enhancing the mass transport of the solvents into the plant cells. The procedure is simple and relatively low cost technology that can be used in both small and larger scale of photochemical extraction. The benefits of UAE are mainly due to reduction in extraction time and solvent consumption. However use of ultrasound energy more than 20KHZ may have an effect on the photo chemicals through the formation of free radicals.

3.2.9. Accelerated Solvent Extraction

Accelerated solvent extraction (ASE) is a way for extracting different chemicals from a complex solid or semisolid model matrix. ASE is a capable from of liquid solvent extraction compared to maceration and soxhlet extraction as this way use the smallest amount of the solvent. Sample is packed with inert material such as sand in the stainless steel extraction cell to prevent sample from aggregating and block the system tubing. Packed SAE cell includes layers of sand sample mixture in between cellulose filter paper and sand layers. The automated extraction technology is able to control temperature and pressure for each individual samples and requires less than an hour for extraction. Similar to other solvent technique, ASE also critically depend on the solvent types.

3.2.10. Supercritical Fluid Extraction

Supercritical fluid is a matter that shares the physical properties of together with gas and liquid at its critical point. Factors such as temperature and pressure are determinates, that push a substance into its region. Supercritical fluid behaves more like a gas other than have the solvating attribution of a liquid.

4. ZnO Nanoparticles

In recent years, increasing attention has been paid to the issue of the biomedical use of metal nanoparticles. Bio safety and the ecological purity of the production of metal nanoparticles, the use of which is growing in many sectors of the economy, is a pressing issue. Chemical and physical methods used to produce nanoparticles are often expensive and not always environmentally friendly. Biological methods are being actively developed as an alternative, effective, cheap, and environmentally friendly solution for the production of nanoparticles with desired properties. Among the organic methods, we can differentiate synthesis using bacteria, yeast, fungi, and plant extracts [7, 8].

5. Methodology

5.1. Dried Plant Leaf

Plants are measured a popular basis of NP synthesis because they allow for the important production of NPs with several shapes and sizes [4] The plant portions manufacturing of ZnO-NPs extracted from flowers or leaves is mainly preserved via existence enclosed in successively tap water and pasteurized double distilled water. The plant helping is then allowed to thirsty at area infection before being balanced and crushed with a mortar and pestle the obligatory total of Milli-Q HO is added to the plant component and boiled under vigorous agitation via a magnetic Stirrer.[5] The plants removals are made by filtration through Whatman filter paper (sample). To confirm effective mixing, the combination is heated to the necessary temperature for the essential time to mix the extract into 0.5 mm of hydrous zinc sulphate or zinc nitrate, or ZnO or solution [6] At this point, approximately experiments were ample with excerpt concentration, temperature, duration, and ph. An incubation period causes the combination to turn yellow as visual resistant of the afresh bent NPs [7]

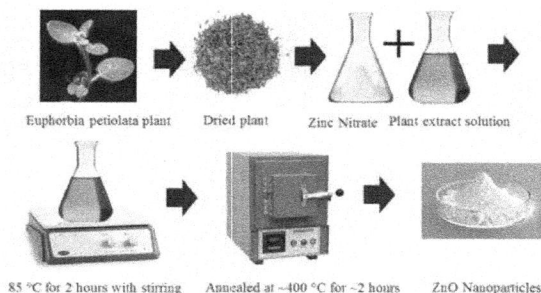

Euphorbia petiolata plant   Dried plant   Zinc Nitrate Plant extract solution

85 °C for 2 hours with stirring   Annealed at ~400 °C for ~2 hours   ZnO Nanoparticles

96

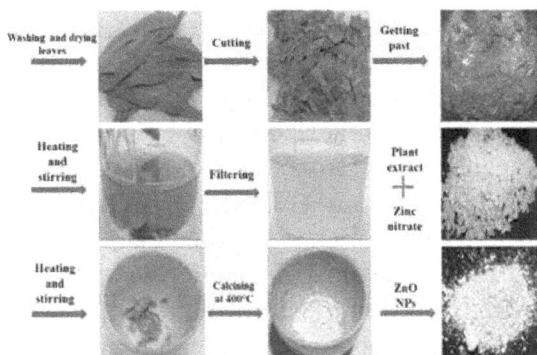

5.2. Fresh Plant Leaves

The collected fresh leaves were washed with distilled water and the leaves cut into small pieces. After that add the small piece of leaves with distilled water were boiled. Then the extract was permitted to cool the normal temperature. After that the extract will be filtered using Whatman filter paper. After that plant extract added with zinc nitrate. Then, 0.049 mol NaOH was dissolved in 25 ml water and slowly the zinc nitrate solution mixer was added. Stirring was done for an hour. After the extract calcinated the extract turns into white color powder. Finally, the ZnO NPs were obtained. [20, 27]

6. Characterization

Characterization of Biosynthesized ZnO NPs. +ermal gravimetric analysis was carried out using a simultaneous DTA-TGA (DTG-60H, Shimadzu Co., Japan) analysis to analyze the decomposition and thermal stability of the biosynthesized ZnO NPs measured at the heating rate of 10°C/min. Crystalline structure and the average crystalline size of the synthesized ZnO NPs were characterized using an X-ray diffractometer (XRD-7000, Shimadzu Co., Japan) equipped with a Cu target for generating a CuKα radiation with λ =1.54056A. XRD spectra were recorded from 10°C to 80°C with 2θ angles using CuKα radiation operated at 40 Kv and 30 mA. The crystallite sizes (D) of the powders were calculated by using Scherrer equation:

$$D = 0.94\lambda / \beta \cos\theta \qquad (1)$$

where K =0.94 is Scherrer constant, λ is the X-ray wavelength, θ is Bragg's diffraction angle, and β is the peak width of the diffraction line at half of the maximum intensity. To analyze the morphology and composition, the biosynthesized ZnO NPs were characterized by field emission scanning electron microscopy equipped with energy dispersive X-ray spectroscopy (FE-SEM, JEOL-JSM 6500F, made in Japan). Furthermore, to analyze the shape, particle size, and crystallinity, the biosynthesized ZnO NPs were characterized using high-resolution transmission electron microscopy (HRTEM, Tecnai F20 G2, Philips, Netherlands) at an accelerating voltage of 200 kV. +e absorption spectra of the biosynthesized ZnO NPs were recorded by using JASCO V-670 UV-Vis spectroscopy equipped with a diffuse reflectance attachment for powder samples in between a wavelength scan of 200 and 800 nm. Biosynthesized ZnO NPs were also characterized using Fourier transform infrared spectroscopy (FTIR, Perkin Elmer 65) to analyze and detect surface functional groups in the scanning range of 4000–400 cm-[1].

7. Survey of Literature

7.1. In, 2022 shayma tahsin karam and Ahmed fattah abdulrahman were reported that, the tried green synthesis of zinc oxide nanoparticles using thyme plant extract., 50 ml thyme leaf extract was added drop wise to the 0.1 m [Zn (NO$_3$)$_2$6H$_2$O] solution 1:1 at room temperature for 1 hr with a magnetic stirrer. Afterward, the leaf extract was well mixed with zinc salt solution to become a homogeneous solution, and the ph of the mixture was regulated and adjusted to ph 8 using sodium hydroxide (NaOH) under magnetic stirring. The color of the combination turned milky white, and then the mixture (solution) was heated at 80 °C for 3 h to obtain a brownish paste. The nucleation and reactivity of the ZnO nanoparticles occur when they form a brownish paste. Lastly, the ZnO powder was calcined (annealed) for 2 hrs at various temperatures of   150 °C, 250 °C, 350 °C, and 450 °C. In addition, the results showed that the variation in calcinations temperature has an important and strong impact on the shape, average size, morphology, crystal quality, optical properties, and energy band gap of ZnO NPs. The FESEM result shows the average size of ZnO NPs was increased from 39.4 nm to 51.86 nm with an increase in the calcinations temperature from 150 °C to 450 °C. The calcinations temperature has a great effect on the crystal size and quality for the hexagonal wurtzite structure of ZnO NPs, and the particle size was increased from 35.202 nm to 43.30 nm with an increase in calcinations temperature. In addition, the FT-IR analysis results at different calcinations temperatures confirm that the ZnO NPs were synthesized with high purity from thyme plant leaf extract. In addition, high absorbance was shown below 400 nm in the UV region, and the visible range had a low absorbance rate. The energy band gap was decreased from 2.7 nm to 2.645 nm with an increase in calcinations temperature. According to the results obtained for the biosynthesized ZnO NPs, the ZnO NPs biosynthesized at the calcinations temperature of 450 °C showed a high quality and improvement compared to the ZnO NPs synthesized at other calcinations temperatures. In addition, the novelty of this study is the green synthesis of ZnO nanoparticles from thyme plant leaf extract, which might be used for photo catalysis, water pollution removal, medicinal (antibacterial) applications, solar cells, and cosmetic applications.[1]

7.2. In, 2021 T.S. Aldeen et al. were reported that, the tried green synthesis of Zinc oxide nanoparticles using Phoenix roebelenii palm leaves. 6.0 g of the zinc precursor salt (Zn $(NO_3)_2.6H_2O$; Fluka, 0.99%) was dissolved in 100 ml of the P. roebelenii extract. The solution was then mixed upon continuous stirring to completely dissolve the Zn salt in the aqueous extract. To complete the reaction, the mixture was covered and left (~20 hrs) at ambient temperature. The resulting brown precipitate was collected via centrifugation. The precipitate was then washed several times with double distilled water and left to dry for 2 hrs in a drying oven at 100 ∘C. The resultant powder was calcined at 500 °C for 2 hrs in a preheated open air tubular furnace. The light-yellow powder of ZnO NPs was ground into a fine powder were obtained and characterized using UV-VIS, FTIR spectrum, XRD and EDX. The pure wurtzite structure of ZnO NPs obtained after calcination at 500 °C was confirmed using XRD. TEM images showed the ZnO NPs were spherical with a particle size distribution between 8 and 25 nm and an average value of 15 ± 0.37 nm. The UV peak at 384.8 nm was due to the NBE transition, while the other emissions are attributed to the structural defects in the ZnO NPS (Zni, VO and Oi). The role of the bioactive compounds of P. roebelenii leaves as an oxidizing agent in the biosynthesis of ZnO has been discussed. The ZnO NPs showed enhanced photo catalytic properties with 89% of MB mineralized after 105 min under UV irradiation. The green synthesized ZnO NPs inhibit the growth of gram-positive and gram-negative pathogenic bacteria. The results of this work highlight the potential of P. roebelenii palm leaves to synthesize multifunctional ZnO NPs used for wastewater treatment and bacterial inactivation.[2]

7.3. In 2020, Barzinjy, A.A., Azeez, H.H. were reported that, the tried green synthesis of Zinc oxide nanoparticles using Eucalyptus globulus Labill. Leaf extract. 20 g of the small pieces of leaves and 5 mL of distilled water were put into a mortar and pastel and crushed into paste. 6 g of this paste was mixed with 100 ml of distilled water in a beaker, after that, 2 Mole of NaOH solutions was added drop wise to regulate the pH of the mixture, observed by a pH meter, to pH 8. Then the mixture was stirred almost continuously for 1 h producing a cloudy precipitous of zinc hydroxide, Zn $(OH)_2$, which was then centrifuged at 5000 rpm for 1 h and dried in an oven set to 60 °C. After that the mixture cooled to room temperature. After preparation of the plant extract as described previously, 30 ml of this extract was put into a beaker and heated gradually. When the temperature reached 60 °C, 3 g of zinc nitrate hexahydrate were added to this extract. After that the mixture was continuously stirred, maintaining the temperature at 60 °C, until the mixture converted into a yellowish paste after 1 h. It is obvious that, the temperature of reaction played important role in producing NPs, the optimal yield of NPs was achieved at 60 °C. Afterward the paste was blazed in a furnace at 400 °C for about 2 hrs then the residual was washed by ethanol and distilled water several times. The powder was then heated at 100 °C to dry. Then zinc oxide nanoparticles were obtained and they were ready for characterization techniques, namely XRD, FE-SEM, EDX, BET, Zeta potential, DLS, differential scanning calorimetric (DSC) analysis, FT-IR analysis and UV–Vis spectroscopy. The utilized green method, in this investigation, provides hexagonal ZnO NPs with average diameter of 35 nm and very high crystallinity. Also, there was an excellent agreement between the particle size measurement using different methods. DSC analysis indicated that, despite the very high crystallinity of the ZnO NPs, the ZnO NPs require additional annealing till about 365 °C in order to be more purified. The biosynthesized ZnO NPs are thermally stable and until 350 °C there was not considerable weight-loss. According to zeta potential analysis the biosynthesized ZnO NPs in this study possess good stability. This result is a good indicator that these nanoparticles possess considerable active adsorption sites to absorb dyes, and heavy metal ions from aqueous systems were not any considerable weight-loss.[4]

7.4. In, 2019 Yeon Jae Shim et al. were reported that, the tried green synthesis of Zinc oxide nanoparticles using S. japonica leaf extract. 5 g of dried stems and leaves of S. japonica were pulverized thoroughly and aut°Claved for 30 min in 100 mL of distil water for synthesis of nanoparticles. After boiling, collected extract (5 %, w/v) was filtered and diluted to reach a concentration of 10 % and stored at 4 °C for further use. The zinc oxide nanoparticles were synthesized by co-precipitation method using zinc nitrate and sodium hydroxide as precursors. Aqueous solution of zinc nitrate (0.1 M) and 10% extract were mixed under constant stirring using a magnetic stirrer. When the solution was heated up to 50°C, sodium hydroxide (0.2 M) was added drop by drop and kept undisturbed for 2 h. After the synthesis, nanoparticles were purified and collected by centrifugation at 5,000 rpm for 10 min, washed thoroughly with sterile water. The washed nanoparticles were kept for 4 hours in 60°C oven and used further for characterization techniques. XRD showed that nanoparticles had hexagonal wurtzite structure with core diameter of around 18nm. UV-Visible spectroscopy (peak at 362 nm) and FTIR (peak at 450 cm^{-1}) confirmed the presence of ZnO in the biosynthesized nanoparticles. The resulting nanoparticles synthesized by S. japonica successfully reduced the toxic methylene blue by 54 %. Synthesized nanoparticles may be a potent photo catalytic material for the degradation of industrial and waste water pollutant methylene blue dye.[5]

7.5. In 2020, M.M. Khan et al. were reported that, the tried green synthesis of ZnO nanoparticles using Costus woodsonii leaf extract. A 30 mL sample of the leaf extract was heated to 60 °C and 3 g of Zn $(NO_3)_2 \cdot 6H_2O$ as a precursor was then added to the reaction chamber. A paste was formed after continuous heating and stirring for ~3 hrs, which was then calcined in a muffle furnace at 400 °C for 2 hrs to form a crystalline powder. The final products were washed several times with ethanol and double distilled water. The dried samples were collected for characterization techniques. XRD confirmed that the as-synthesized ZnO NPs were hexagonal wurtzite in structure and crystalline. The optical band gaps of ZnO-C and as-synthesized ZnO NPs (ZnO-UL1and ZnO-BL1) were 3.18 eV, ~2.68 eV, and ~2.77 eV, respectively. FTIR spectroscopy confirmed the synthesis of ZnO with the coating or wrapping of the as-synthesized ZnO NPs with some organic compounds from the leaf extract of plant Costus woodsonii. XPS confirmed that the chemical state of Zn was Zn^{2+}, and VB-XPS revealed band gap lowing of the as-synthesized ZnO NPs. This green approach for the synthesis of narrow band gap ZnO NPs.[6]

7.6. In 2020, Jayappa, M. D., Ramaiah, C. K., Kumar, M. A. P., Suresh, D., Prabhu, A., Devasya, R. P., & Sheikh, S. were reported that, the tried green synthesis of ZnO nanoparticles using callus of Mussaenda frondosa L. Two grams of plant extract was dissolved in 100 ml dH2O with continuous stirring on a magnetic stirrer (450 to 500 rpm) for about 15 min. The stoichiometric amount of Zn $(NO_3)_2 \cdot 6H_2O$ was dispersed in a known amount of combustible fuel to make a reaction mixture and kept in a preheated muffle furnace for combustion at 400 °C for 10–30 min. synthesized nanoparticles using for characterization techniques. XRD study showed wurtzite structures of ZnO-NPs. The average crystallite size of synthesized semiconductor ZnO-NPs was found in the range of 5-25 nm. The UV–Vis spectral analysis confirmed that the maximum absorption at 370–376 nm range corresponds to the intrinsic band gap of ZnO-NPs. SEM images confirmed the spongy structure of agglomerated spherical-shaped nanoparticles. FTIR spectra revealed the absorption bands between 3350 and 1045 cm^{-1}, confirming the stretching of functional groups involved in the bio reduction of

ZnO-NPs. DLS analysis unveiled the monodispersed and stability of bio reduced nanoparticles. Carcinogenic methylene blue dye was efficiently disintegrated using ZnO-NPs under UV light. In addition, the present work also demonstrated a significant antioxidant, anti-inflammatory, antidiabetic and anticancer activities of ZnO-NPs.[7]

7.7. In 2021, N. M. Salem and A.M. Awwad were reported that, the tried green synthesis of ZnO nanoparticles using Solanum rantonnetii leaves aqueous extract. A 10g of zinc acetate dihydrate Zn $(CH_3COO)_2.2H_2O$ was dissolved in 100 ml de-ionized water under stirring with magnetic bar at ambient temperature (27 °C). Afterward, an aqueous extract of S.rantonnetii leaves aqueous extract was added drop by drop to zinc solution till the solution started changing from colorless color to white and the formation of suspended particles. The mixture was left overnight and filtered to obtain the suspended particles, which dried in an oven at 80 °C for 4hrs. The powder obtained was subjected to analysis by different characterizations. X-ray diffraction (XRD) pattern of the ZnO NPs agrees with the reported data for Zn metal and the crystallite average size is 12 nm. UV–vis absorption spectra for surface Plasmon resonance (SPR) peak (~374 nm). Scanning and transmission electron microscopic (SEM and TEM) show uniform spherical particles obtained by this green method. The antifungal activity is found to be effective of ZnO NPs. Results revealed that the green synthesis is an efficient for the preparation of ZnO NPs as an active antifungal agent for practical applications.[9]

7.8. In 2015, T. Bhuyan et al. were reported that, tried green synthesis of ZnO nanoparticles using Azadirachta indica (Neem) leaf extract, Zinc acetate dehydrate $[(CH_3COO)_2.2H_2O]$ and sodium hydroxide (NaOH) were used as the starting material. Briefly, zinc acetate (2 M) was prepared in 50 ml of deionized water under constant stirring conditions. After complete dissolution of the mixture, 1 ml of 25% leaf extract and 50 ml of 2 M NaOH were added to the prepared solution of zinc acetate. The mixture was stirred continuously for 2 h on magnetic stirrer resulting in white precipitate. The precipitate was filtered and washed with distilled water followed by ethanol in order to remove the impurities. Finally, a white powder was obtained after overnight drying of the purified precipitate at 60 °C in oven overnight. The obtained nanoparticles used for different characterizations. The XRD patterns showing strong and narrow diffraction peaks indicate that the zinc oxide nanoparticles synthesized are crystalline in nature. The average particle size of the nanostructures was around 8.4 nm. UV–visible absorption spectra were evaluated by UV–visible spectroscopy in the wavelength range of 300–800 nm. UV–Vis absorption spectra of biosynthesized ZnO nanoparticles sample exhibiting absorption peak at 377 nm. The FTIR spectrum showed bands at 713 and 844 cm^{-1} corresponding to the C–H stretching of alkanes, C–H (aromatics) and –OH stretching of intramolecular H-bond, C– C stretching of alkanes . Biologically synthesized ZnO nanoparticles can act as an effective antimicrobial and photo catalytic agent[14].

7.9 In 2019, H Chemingui *et al.* were reported that, tried green synthesis of ZnO nanoparticles using Laurus nobilis leaf extract. 20 ml of L. nobilis leaves extract was heated at 80 by using a stirrer-heater. Five grams of zinc nitrate hexahydrate (Zn $(NO_3)_2.6H_2O$, Sigma Aldrich (AR)) was added to the extract solution until the temperatures reached 80 °C[23]. This paste was later collected in a ceramic crucible and heated in an air-heated furnace at 400 °Cfor 3 h. A light yellow powder was obtained and this powder was carefully collected and used for different characterizations. The XRD shows that the size of nanoparticles ranges between 20 to 30 nm. FT-IR studies clearly showed the formation of ZnO and indicated that the plant contains flavones and phenol, which work as capping and reducing agents for the synthesis of spherical ZnO NPs. The ZnO NPs were proved as an effective antibacterial agent against Escherichia Coli. This study demonstrated the enhanced photo catalytic properties of biosynthesized ZnO by comparing with the commercial ZnO NPs.[15]

7.10. In 2020, Meron Girma Demissie et al. were reported that, the tried green synthesis of ZnO nanoparticles using Lippia adoensis leaf extract. 1: 1 (50 ml Lippia adoensis extract and 50 ml of 0.45 M zinc acetate dihydrate), 3: 2 (60 ml Lippia adoensis extract and 40 ml of 0.45 M zinc acetate dihydrate), and 9 : 1 (90 ml Lippia adoensis extract and 10 ml of 0.45 M zinc acetate dihydrate) ratios were mixed with 50 ml, 40 ml, and 10 ml of 0.45 M NaOH, respectively. The three mixtures were then stirred continuously for 2 hrs using a magnetic stirrer at 800 rpm that resulted in yellow precipitate formation. The precipitates were then filtered using a glass filter and washed repeatedly with distilled water followed by ethanol in order to remove the impurities and oven dried at 100 °C for 1 hr. The obtained dried light yellow color powders were mashed using a mortar and pestle. Finally, after conducting thermal stability of the biosynthesized nanoparticles, the mashed yellow powders were calcined at 400 °C for 1 hr and fine ground and made ready for further characterizations. XRD analysis showed that the average crystal sizes of ZnO NPs synthesized from 3 : 2, 1 : 1, and 9 : 1 ratios by volume were found to be 22.6 nm, 18.5 nm, and 26.8 nm. SEM and TEM analysis showed that the morphology of the biosynthesized ZnO NPs was predominantly spherical in shape even though nanorod-shaped structures were also observed. Furthermore, the purity of the ZnO NPs was also confirmed from EDS analysis. The optical band-gap energies were determined from UV-Vis using the Tauc plot and found to be 3.11, 3.21, and 3.05 eV for ZnO NPs synthesized from 3 : 2, 1 : 1, and 9 : 1 ratios by volume, respectively. Further, the biosynthesized ZnO nanoparticles using Lippia adensis leaf extract have proved themselves to be an effective antibacterial agent against both Gram-positive (S. aureus and E. feacalis) and Gram-negative (E. coli and K. pneumonia) bacteria[16].

7.11. In 2019, S.S. Rad, et al. were reported that, the tried green synthesis of ZnO nanoparticles using leaf extract of Mentha pulegium L. The weighed of 5 g powder leaf were boiled with 100 ml of deionized water for 10 min at 60 °C and filtered through Whatman No.1 filter paper. Further, 20 ml of Mentha pulegium leaf aqueous extract boiled at 60–80 °C by using magnetic stirrer. When the temperature of the solution was reached at 60°C, 2 g of zinc nitrate hexahydrate (Zn $(NO_3)_2 \cdot 6H_2O$) was added and allowed to boil until the extract became a paste. Afterwards it transferred to a ceramic crucible cup and heated in furnace at 400 °C for 2 hrs. This powdered product (ZnO NPs) was used for the further studies. The

XRD data showed the crystalline nature of the nanoparticles and EDX measurements indicated the high zinc content of 56.26% and also oxygen with 43.74%. FT-IR confirmed the presence of functional groups of both leaf extract and ZnO NPs. The particles size and morphology determined from FE-SEM and TEM. UV visible absorbance spectrum of ZnO NPs exhibited the absorbance band at 370 nm. The synthesized ZnO nanoparticles as potential antibacterial agent has been studied on Escherichia coli and Staphyloc occus aureus. These results indicate that aqueous extract of Mentha pulegium are effective reducing agents for green synthesis of ZnO NPs with significant antimicrobial potential.[17]

7.12. In 2021, Rouhina Saemi , et al. were reported that, the tried green synthesis of ZnO nanoparticles using Walnut leaf extract $Zn(NO_3)_3 \cdot 6H_2O$ was dissolved in 20 ml of the walnut leaf extract and volume up to 50 ml by DI double distilled water. The solution was placed on a stirrer at 60 °C for various duration (30– 90 min). The prepared solution was heated in a furnace at 400 °C for 2 h. Finally, white colored powder was obtained. This powdered product was utilized for further investigation of the XRD peaks shows that average crystal size of the sample was discovered to be 38 nm. The FT-IR spectrum of the extract of walnut leaves revealed some peaks at 2,921, 2,356, 1,569, 1,457, 1,305, and 674 cm^{-1}. SEM displayed that the synthesized ZnO NPs were of small particle size with narrow size distribution. . The formed ZnO NPs and the ZnO NPs incorporated polyethylene films displayed significant antibacterial activity against E. coli[18].

7.13. In 2020, Naseer, M., Aslam, U., Khalid, B. et al. were reported that, the green route to synthesize Zinc Oxide Nanoparticles using leaf extracts of Cassia fistula and Melia azadarach . 0.01M zinc acetate dihydrate (Zn $(C_2H_3O_2)_2.2H_2O$) solution was prepared in H_2O. For synthesis of ZnO nanoparticles, 95ml of 0.01M zinc acetate dihydrate (Zn $(C_2H_3O_2)_2.2H_2O$) solution was mixed separately with 5ml plant extract. These mixtures were incubated at 70°Cfor 1hour with continuous shaking at 150 rpm. This led to the settlement of bio-reduced salt at the bottom of the flask which appeared as white precipitate. The supernatant was decanted and powdery precipitate was transferred to 1.5 ml centrifuge tubes. Both the samples were subjected to washing with deionized H_2O by centrifugation at 3000 rpm for 30 minutes. Washing step was repeated thrice to ensure removal of impurities. The UV-Vis shows that maximum absorption peak for ZnO NPs was recorded at 320 nm. XRD results gives that the particle size of the ZnO NPs was 2.72 nm. FTIR spectrometry was performed. Spectral peaks at 683–500 cm^{-1} and 698–505 cm^{-1} proposed the formation of ZnO nanoparticles. Antibacterial analysis revealed that ZnO NPs synthesized from leaf extracts exhibited significant capability of inhibition against the clinical pathogens when compared to traditional drugs.[19]

7.14. In 2020, S. Sheik Mydeen, R. Raj Kumar, M. Kottaisamy, V.S. Vasantha, were reported that, Biosynthesis of ZnO nanoparticles through extract from Prosopis juliflora plant leaf, $Zn(CH_3COO)_2 \cdot 2H_2O$, 0.024 mole was dissolved in 30ml double distilled water and mixed with 0.0005 mole Tetra decyl trimethyl ammonium bromide (TTAB). Then, it was kept in 1h stirrer by adding 1ml of leaf extract. Then, 0.049 mole NaOH was dissolved in 25ml water and slowly the zinc acetate solution mixer was added. Stirring was done for an hour. The zinc acetate solution mixer was taken into a Teflon Aut°Clave and heated for 5hours in 170°C. The resulting white color precipitate was filtered and washed with distilled water and ethanol many times. In few hours, it was dehydrated at 60°C. The dried precipitate was collected and ground using an agate mortar. Ultimately, the synthesized nanoparticle was annealed at 350°C in a muffle furnace for 2 hours and then allowed for cooling. The obtained powder used for further characterizations. The XRD has confirmed that the ZCA and ZLE nanoparticles are found to have the hexagonal wurtzite structure with absorption bands in FT-IR maximum at 474cm^{-1}. The average crystallite sizes of titled ZCA and ZLE nanoparticles crystalline were ranged from 31 to 32 nm. PL spectra have shown green emission peak intensity and explained the minimum defect in the surface area of crystal. UV–Visible diffuse reflectance spectrum has exhibited that the energy band different values are 3.23 and 3.25eV. ZnO-Rust still remains at high photo catalytic activity and also possesses stability for a long time.[20]

7.15. In 2017, J. Santhoshkumar, S. VenkatKumar, S.Rajeshkumar were reported that, the tried green synthesis of ZnO nanoparticles using Passiflora caerulea fresh leaf extract. 1 mM Zinc acetate $[Zn(O_2CCH_3)_2(H_2O)_2]$ was dissolved in 50 ml Milli-Q water and kept in stirrer for 1 h respectively. Then 20 ml of NaOH solution was slowly added into the Zinc acetate solution and 25 ml of plant extract was added to the same. The color of the reaction mixture was changed after 1 hrs of incubation time. The solution was left in stirrer for 3 hrs Yellow color appeared after the incubation time confirmed the synthesis of ZnO NPs. The XRD analysis proved the crystalline nature of the ZnO NP. EDX analysis confirmed the presence of zinc and oxide ions in the nanoparticles. UV-Visible spectroscopy at a maximum absorbance is 380 nm. The anti-bacterial activity of ZnO NPs has proved that these can be used as potent anti-bacterial agent against urinary tract infection[22].

7.16. In 2016, S. Vijayakumar et al. were reported that, the tried green synthesis of ZnO nanoparticles using the aqueous leaf extract of Laurus nobilis. Zinc acetate dehydrate $[Zn(CH_3COO)_2]2H_2O$ and sodium hydroxide (NaOH) were used as the starting material. Briefly, zinc acetate (2 M) was prepared in 50 ml of deionized water under constant stirring. After complete dissolution of the mixture, 5 ml of leaf extract and 50 ml of 2 M NaOH were added to the prepared solution of zinc acetate. The mixture was kept under magnetic stirrer for 2 h. The resultant white precipitate was filtered and washed repeatedly with distilled water followed by ethanol to remove the impurities. Finally, a solid white powder was obtained after overnight drying of the purified precipitate at 60 °C in an oven. The powder was then subjected to calcination under muffle furnace at 350 °C for 3 hrs. the XRD shows that Ln-ZnO NPs were crystalline in nature, flower like and have hexagonal wurtzite structure with a mean particle size of 47.27 nm. FTIR spectra of Ln-ZnO NPs were in the range of 500–4000 cm^{-1}. The particle size distribution EDX and SEM shows of Ln-ZnO NPs ranged from 34.5, 52.28 and 55.03 nm by area, perimeter and dimensions respectively with a mean size of 47.27 nm. . The green synthesized

Ln-ZnO NPs has greater antibacterial and antibiofilm activity against Gram positive (S.aureus) and Gram negative (P. aeruginosa) bacteria.

7.17. In 2021, A. Jayachandran et al. were reported that, the tried green synthesis of ZnO nanoparticles using Cayratia pedata leaf extract. . 5 ml of 10 mM Zn $(NO3)2.6H2O$ was poured into the homogeneous leaf extracts prepared, and the mixture is stirred at 65 °C for 20 min. Both sample A and sample B. having turned light yellow were then collected and allowed to heat overnight at the same temperature until a thick yellow paste was obtained. This paste was then dried completely and calcined at 400 °C for 2 hrs before collecting and packing separately for further characterization. Calcination removes the impurities present in the sample, and you get a purified form of the NP, and the press is temperature-dependent. This process was repeated for 55 °C and 75 °C, temperatures above and below the working temperature. While experimenting with 55 °C, the reaction between Zinc Nitrate and plant extract was not happening, resulting in nano ZnO formation. Moreover, when used 75 °C as the working temperature, it formed ashes because the temperature was too high. However, at 65 °C, a yellow color change was observed without any side effects. Moreover, while doing characterization, the sample was confirmed to be ZnO nanoparticles. Hence the temperature plays an important role in the formation of nanoparticles. The various stages of ZnO nanoparticle synthesis using the plant extract of Cayratia pedata. XRD shows that average size was found to be 52.24 nm. Composition was determined by EDX studies. The stretching and bonding were examined through FT-IR spectroscopy, and the shape and average size of the nanoparticles formed were investigated using XRD analysis. The synthesized ZnO nanoparticles gave a relative activity of 60% when used for enzyme immobilization, which is 88.2% of the activity compared to native ZnO immobilization.[24]

7.18. In 2022, K. Dulta et al. were reported that, the tried green synthesis of ZnO nanoparticles using Carica papaya leaf extract. 50 ml 0.1 M Zinc acetate dihydrate was prepared in double distilled water. 10 ml of C.papaya leaf extract was slowly added drop wise to the solution at   80 °C under magnetic stirring for 4 hrs, adjusted to pH 12. The resulting mixture was centrifuged at 10,000 rpm for 10 min. the pellet was washed and centrifuged at 5000 rpm for 10 min. The washed pellet obtained after centrifugation was dried at 50 °C for 6 hrs and calcined in a muffle furnace at 450 °C to synthesize zinc oxide NPs. The synthesize nanoparticles used for further characterizations. XRD shows that average size of the nanoparticles obtained was measured as 14 nm. The absorption spectrum of the synthesized zinc oxide NPs by C.papaya leaf extract showed max optical absorption bands at 360 nm. EDX confirms the presence of zinc and oxygen signals of zinc oxide nanoparticles. The elemental analysis of the nanoparticle yielded 78.58% of zinc and 21.42% of oxygen which proves that the produced nanoparticle is in its highest purified form. Antioxidant activity of ZnO NPs was evaluated by ABTS and DPPH scavenging analysis. . In antifungal study, it was reported that synthesized ZnO nanoparticles showed antifungal effect against Sclerotinia sclerotiorum, Rosellinia necatrix and Fusarium spp. When looking at the effect of ZnO nanoparticles on seed germination, 75% of zinc oxide nanoparticles is most suitable for improving the root and shoot length.[27]

7.19. In 2011, G. Sangeetha et al. were reported that, the tried green synthesis of ZnO nanparticles using aloe Vera leaf extract. 250 g portion of thoroughly washed Aloe Vera leaves were finely cut and boiled with de-ionized water in medium flame. The resulting product was ground to get complete extract. The solution was boiled, filtered and stored in refrigerator for further experiments. In the second process, the inner gel portion was extracted from the aloe leaves, crushed and ground to thin paste by adding enough de-ionized water and filtered by using fine mesh. The resulting extract was stored at 10 °C for further experiments. In synthesis, zinc nitrate was dissolved in distilled water under constant stirring. While at room temperature, sodium hydroxide solution was added drop by drop. After completion of reaction, the solution was allowed to settle for overnight and the supernatant liquid was discarded. The white precipitate formed was washed thoroughly with double distilled water to remove all the ions and then centrifuged at 3000 rpm for 10 min. The obtained precipitate was dried in a hot air oven at 80°C for 6 hrs. the obtained powder used for further characterizations. SEM and TEM analysis shows that the zinc oxide nanoparticles prepared were poly dispersed and the average size ranged from 25 to 40 nm.

UV absorption spectra with the absorption peak ranging from 358 to 375 nm. FT-IR spectra show that ZnO absorption band near 528 cm^{-1}. Zinc oxide nanoparticles prepared from Aloe Vera leaf broth are expected to have more extensive applications in biomedical fields and in cosmetic industries.[28]

8. Conclusion

Green synthesis of metal and metal oxide nanoparticles has been an extremely striking research part finished the last decade. Frequent types of ordinary citations (i.e., bio components like plant, bacteria, fungi, yeast, and plant extract) have been employed as effective possessions for the mixture and fabrication of materials. Among them, plant extract has been established to possess high efficacy as steadying and falling representatives for the synthesis of measure materials. Expansion of potential 'green' materials nanoparticle synthesis should be absorbed near spreading laboratory-based work to a manufacturing scale by since traditional present problems, particularly health and environmental belongings. Yet, 'green' material nanoparticle synthesis originated on bio component - derived resources nanoparticles is probable to be applied lengthily both in the ground of environmental remediation and in other significant areas like pharmaceutical, food, and cosmetic industries. Biosynthesis of metals and their oxide materials nanoparticles using marine algae and marine plants is a part that remainders mainly unexplored.

Consequently, ample possibilities remain for the exploration of new green preparatory strategies based on biogenic synthesis. The future expectations from the green route of nanoparticles synthesis are that the applications of these will grow exponentially, but there is a need to concern about the long-term effects of these on animal and human being as well as accumulation of these in the environment is a subject of worry which has to be resolved in future. These biogenic nanoparticles can be used in nano weapons against phytopathogens as well as in the disinfection of water in various forms for environmental remediation. In the drug delivery system, these nanoparticles might be the future thrust for the biomedical field.

References :
1. Karam, S.T., Abdulrahman, A.F., *Photonics* 2022, 9, 594
2. Aldeen, T.S., Mohamed, H.E.A., Maaza, M., *J. Phys. Chem. Solids* 2022, 160,110313.
3. Barzinjy, A.A., Hamad, S.M., Abdulrahman, A.F., Biro, S.J., Ghafor, A.A., *Curr. Org. Synth.,* 17, 558 (2020).
4. Barzinjy, A.A.; Azeez, H.H., *Appl. Sci.,* 2, 991 (2020).
5. Shim, Y.J., *Optik*, 182, 1015 (2019).
6. Khan, M.M., Saadah, N.H., Harunsani, M.H.; Tan, A.L., Cho M.H., *Mater. Sci. Semicond.Process.*, 91, 194 (2019).
7. Jayappa, M.D., Ramaiah, C.K., Kumar, M.A.P., *Appl Nanosci.,* 10, 3057 (2020).
8. Aman Gour, Narendra Kumar Jain, *Nanomedicine and Biotechnology*, 47:1, 844 (2019).
9. NM. Salem, A.M. Awwad.Green, *Chemistry International*, 8(1), 12 (2022).
10. Khadeeja Parveen, Viktoria Banse, and Lalita Ledwani, *AIP Conference Proceeding,* 1724, 020048 (2016).
11. Irfan Ijaz, Ezaz Gilani, Ammara Nazir, Aysha Bukhari, *Green Chemistry Letters and Reviews,*13:3, 223 (2020).
12. Anu Rana, Krishna Yadav, Sheeja Jagadevan, *Journal of Cleaner Production,* 272,122880 (2020).
13. Salem, S.S., Fouda, A., *Biol Trace Elem Res.,* 199, 344 (2021).
14. Bhuyan, T., Mishra, K., Khanuja, M., Prasad, R., *Materials Science in Semiconductors Processing,* 32, 55 (2015).
15. Chemingui H, Missaoui T, Mzali J.C, Yildiz T, Konyar M, Smiri M, Saidi, N, Hafiane, A, Yatmaz H.C, *Mater. Res. Express,* 6, 1050b4 (2019).
16. Demissie M.G, Sabir F.K, Edossa G.D, Gonfa B.A, *Journal of Chemistry,* 1 (2020).
17. Rad S.S, Sani A.M, Mohseni S, *Microbial Pathogenesis*, 131, 239 (2019).
18. Saemi R, Taghavi E, Jafarizadeh-Malmiri H, Anarjan N, *Green Processing and Synthesis*, 10, 112 (2021).
19. Naseer M, Aslam U, Khalid B, Chen B, *Sci Rep.,* 10, 9055 (2020).
20. Mydeen S.S, Kumar R.R, Kottaisamy M, Vasantha V.S, *Journal of Saudi Chemical Society,* 24, 393 (2020).

21. Ahmed S, Annu, Chaudhry S. A, Ikram S, *Journal of Photochemistry and Potobiology B: Biology*, 166, 272 (2017).
22. Santhoshkumar J, Venkat Kumar S, Rajeshkumar S, *Resour. Efficient Technol.*, 3, 459 (2017).
23. Sekar V, Baskaralingam V, Balasubramanian M, Malaikkarasu S, *Biomed Pharmacother*, 84,1213 (2016).
24. Jayachandran A, Nair A. S, *Biochemistry and Biophysics Reports*, 26, 100995 (2021).
25. M. Raafat, A. S. A. el-Sayed, and M. T. el-Sayed, *Molecules*, 26, 2290 (2021).
26. Asemani M, Anarjan N, *Green Processing and Synthesis*, 8, 557 (2019).
27. Dulta K., Koşarsoy Ağçeli G., Chauhan P., Jasrotia R., Chauhan P.K, *J Clust Sci.*, 33, 603 (2022).
28. G. Sangeetha, S. Rajeshwari, and R. Venckatesh, *Mater. Res. Bull.*, 46, 2560 (2011).
29. A. Singh, N. B. Singh, I. Hussain, H. Singh, V. Yadav, and S. C. Singh, *J. Biotechnol.*, 233, 84 (2016).
30. Subramanian Ambika, Mahalingam Sundararajan, *Journal of Photochemistry and Photobiology B: Biology*, 146, 1011 (2015).

[1]**Department of physics,**
School of basic science ,
Vels institute of science technology and advanced studies,
Chennai, India
[2]**Department of BioEngineering,**
School of Engineering ,
Vels institute of science technology and advanced studies,
Chennai, India
Corresponding author : gowthamivijayakumar@gmail.com

13. Deserted Wild Plant of Immense Medicinal Importance : Solanum xanthocarpum Schrad & Wendl.

Dr. Kritika Jyoti Namdeo

Abstract

Solanum xanthocarpum Belongs to family Solanaceae an important medicinal herb in ayurvedic and mordern industry. It is a diffuse prickly herb that is immensely important (one of the members of Dasamula of the Ayurveda) in traditional system of medicine apart from possessing various potential uses including eco-friendly attributes. It is found throughout India mostly in dry places as a common weed on roadsides and waste lands. The all parts of the plants are medicinally important. It has been used for treatment of many infectious and degenerative diseases in traditional medicine. The species contain steroids, alkaloids, solasonine and solamargin Solasonin serves as an important intermediate in the synthesis of steroidal hormones.

According to recent history this plant is reported for various medicinal properties such as antifertility, anathematic, antifilarial and mosquito larvicidal activity. Apigenin and solamargine exhibited anticancer property. It is particularly effective against lung cancer and colon cancer. In Ayurveda, plant is described as pungent, bitter, digestive, alternative astringent. Stems, flowers, fruits are bitter and contains carminative properties and also used as febrifuge, effective diuretic and expectorant. So, the whole plant is used traditionally for curing various ailments (Atul et al.,2013). This is an urgent need to meet the ever-growing demand of medicinal plants in the market and it will pose a challenge for researchers' farmers, conservationist and policy makers to manage and use our natural resources wisely.

Keywords : Solanum xanthocarpum, larvicidal properties, solasomargine.

Introduction

Herbal medicines are being used by nearly about 80% of the world population, primarily in developing countries for primary health care

In the 17th The literature survey reveals that the plants have been used by the people from time immemorial. Ancient literature is full of text about plant uses. The earliest known record of plant being used in medication is found on an Egyption papyrus dated about 1550 B.C. Since then, plants have provided successfully nearly half of the worlds, drugs. Written records of the use of plant for curing human or animal disease in India can be traced back to the earliest (1500-1600 B.C.), scripture of the Hindus, the Rigveda. In India, the Ayurvedic system of medicine have been in use for over 3000 years. Charak (900-800 B.C.) and Susruta, (400 A.D.) two of the earliest Indian prodigies had written Charak Samhita and Susruta Samhita respectively these books are esteemed even to this day as the treasure of literature on indigenous medicine. "The Herbal" by Gerade in 1633 appeared on medicinal plants. century most prolific writer was Bahunin (1623). As early as 1918, Basu compiled "Indian medicinal plants" which he revised with Kirtikar (1935) in 4 volumes. Between 1948 and 1966 was published "The Wealth of India, Raw materials" by CSIR in several volumes by eminent Indian authors

The plant is found in all districts in plants and low hills through India. Tropical and sub tropical reagions of the world common in waste places, river beds and in cultivation the species adopted in wet to extremes dry condition. Two varieties of Kantakari are mentioned in the text viz. the blue flowered and the white flowered ones, of which the blue flowered is more common. In practice, the blue flowered Solanum surattense Burm. F. (Solanaceae) is being used as drug sources in Kerala.

The plant is very diffuse, bright green perennial herb, woody at the base. Stem somewhat zigzag, sparsely or densely clothed with stellate tomentum when young, at length glabrous. The leaves are ovate or elliptic in outline, sinuate or sub pinnatifid obtuse or subacute, stellately hairy on both surface (specially beneath), rarely becoming glabrous with age, both surfaces armed with long. yellow, sharp prickles on the midrib and nerves, the latter raised on the lower surface, the base usually unequal sided, petiole 3-7 cm long, prickly and stellately hairy, decurrent at the base into 2 ridges running down to the next lower node. The flowers are in 2-6 flowered cymose inflorescence. The calyx is 0.6cm long, aculeate and stellate hairy. The corolla is blue and lobes shallow. The fruits are globose berries about 1.5 cm long and yellow when ripe. The seeds are 0.2 cm x 0.1 cm and glabrous. Flowering and fruiting is March-June.

Synonyms :

Solanum surratense Burm. f.; Solanum maccani Sant; Solanion virginianum Linn.

Vernacular Names :

Latin : Solanum surattense, Syn. S. Xanthocarpum

Hindi : Bhatkatiya, Kately Baigan, Kately, ringani.

Sanskrit : Kantakari, pusparsa, Vyaghri, Dravini, Nindigdhika, Ksudrakantaka.Ksudraphala, duh. Praharsini,Pracodani, Bahukanta, Bahugudakulas, Vartaki, Rastriki.

Bengali : Kantakari.

Marathi : Bhuiringani

Tamil : Kantankattiri

 Malayalam : Kantkariccunta, Kantakarivalutana, Kantankattiti

Oriya : Bhejibegun, ankranti.

Pungabi : Kandyali, Mahori, Warumba.

Bihaar : Rangnie, Bhat-khataya, Rangaini, Janum.

Telugu : Callamulaga, Pinnamulaka, Nelamulaka, Vakudu Kannad: Nelagulle

Tribal Name : Baigan, vegi-baigan, Ramgani (Lo.); Rambaigan.(Sa).

Chemical Constituents in Plants :

Solanum xanthocarpum has a high concentration of solasodine alkaloid, a spiroketal alkaloid sapogenin with a heterocyclic nitrogen atom, which is the starting material for the manufacture of cortisone and sex hormones.

The fruit contain ß-carotene, caffeic, chlorgenic, isochlorogenic and neochlorogenic acids, esculin, esculatin, scopoletin, cycloartanol, cycloartenol, chlosterol, diosgenin, carpesterol, solsodine solamargine, B-solamargine, solasonine, L-rhamnosyl- B-D-glucoside, B- sitosterol and stigmastery glucoside, arachidic, linoleic, oleic, palmitic and stereric acids and solanocarpine from the fruit oil and heteroside of tomatidienol from fruit stalk have been isolated. The flower contains diosgenin, apigenin and quercetin-3-0-B- glupyranosyl-O-B-mannopyranoside. (Chatterjee and Pakrashi, 1955). Several steroidal saponins, steroidal alkaloids, disaccharides, flavonoids, and phenols have been implicated in the biological activities.The berries are the main source of solasodine and diosgenin. Solasodine is N-analogue of diosgenin and used as a steroidal precursor in the steroid drug industry for the manufacture of corticosteroids, antifertility drugs, anabolic steroids etc. It is present in the form of a glycoside in most of the berries of the plant belonging to the genus solanum and the glycoalkaloids are variously known as solasonine, solamargine etc. with the common spiro aminoketal alkaloid or aglycon namely solasodine. The solasodine content of the berries of solanum xanthocarpum is reported to vary from 1.1% to 4.6% depending apparently on climatic and soil conditions. It has been observed that berries collected in autumn (September, October) yielded only solasonine and solamargine without any trace of solasurine which was obtained from the material collected in summer (May, June). The solasodine content of the unripe berries was 1.7% (on dry weight basis) as against 0.75% noted for the ripe berries.

Traditional Uses

Lodhas give root paste with honey (3:1) to patient during fever for stopping vomiting. They prescribe root decoction with paste of long pepper (3:2) as antidote to pox. Leaf decoction of long pepper with paste of ginger (3:2) to patient suffering from dengu fever and advise to smoke dried seed powder for treatment of asthma.

Mundas apply root paste as cure for scabies. Oraons give fruit paste with leaf juice of Shorea robusta and common salt (5:3:1) to children against whooping cough. Seed paste with paste of Peaju (Allium cepa) (5:2) as cure for toothache. The fresh flower pastes as balm on watery erupton on skins. They give 10 fried fruits as cure for cough and cold. The plant is also known to have pest repellent properties and used as a contact poison and mollusicide. Roots are one of the constituents of well-known Ayurvedic preparation

"Dasmul Asava" and used as an expectorant, cough, asthma, and chest pain in Ayurvedic medicine.

Fruits are edible and used by the local people as folk medicines in treating throat infections and other inflammatory problems. The stem, flowers and fruits are prescribed for relief in burning sensation in the feet accompanied by vesicular eruptions. The antispasmodic, antitumor, cardiotonic, hypotensive, antianaphylactic and cytotoxic activities are also reported Fruit juice is useful in sore throats and rheumatism. A decoction of the fruits of the plant is used by tribal and rural people of Orissa, India for the treatment of diabetes. The fruits are eaten as an anthelmintic and for indigestion.

Veterinary: Lodhas put juice of flower as cure for watery eyes of cattle and also apply fresh fruit paste for treatment of foot sore.

Medicinal Uses :

According to the Chatterjee and Pakrashi (1995), the whole plant is alterative, antiasthmatic, astringent, digestive, febrifuge, bitter and pungent. It is used in bronchitis, cough, dropsy and constipation. A decoction of the plant is given in gonorrhea and to promote conception. The fruits flower and stems are bitter and carminative and are prescribed in ignipetidites associated with a vesicular and watery eruption. The vapour of burning seeds are used as an expectorant in asthma, cough and in toothache. The leaves are considered anodyne and their juice with black pepper is prescribed in rheumatism. (Chopra et al.1996). Root is pungent, bitter, heating appetizer, laxative, stomachic, anthelmintic, diuretic, expectorant, febrifuge and aphrodisiac, useful in asthma, bronchitis, fever, lumbago pains, piles, urinary concretion, and disease of heart, and also one of the constituents of Sashamula Asava".

Pharmacological Actions

Solanum xanthocarpum is widely used by practitioners of the Siddha system of medicine in southern India to treat respiratory diseases. The powder of whole dried plant or a decoction is used for this purpose. Govindan et al. (1999) showed that treatment with solanum xanthocarpum improved the pulmonary functions to a significant level in patients suffering from mild to moderate asthma. The dose of solanum xanthocarpum was well tolerated and no untoward effects were reported. solanum xanthocarpum is a safe medicine in the traditional system and has been used by mankind over many centuries. It was suggested that relief from the symptoms of bronchial asthma produced by plant may be due to:(a) a bronchodilator effect, (b) reduction in the bronchial mucosal edema, and/or (c) reduction in the secretions within the airway lumen. Antiasthmatic properties Bronchial asthma is an inflammatory disorder of the airways characterized by various airway obstruction, airway eosinophilic inflammation and bronchial hyper responsiveness and is a global health problem that results from a complex interplay between genetic and environmental factors . Among several respiratory diseases affecting man, bronchial asthma is the most common disabling syndrome. Nearly 7–10% of the world population suffers from bronchial asthma. Despite the availability of a wide range of drugs, the relief offered by them is mainly symptomatic and short lived. Moreover, the side effects of these drugs are ongoing to identify effective and safe remedies to treat bronchial asthma. A pilot study on the clinical efficacy of solanum xanthocarpum and Solanum trilobatum in bronchial asthma were undertaken to prove the significant use of herbs in treatment of asthma. Major literature data supports use of whole plants. Gautam et al. (2008) evaluated the therapeutic effect of ethanolic extract of solanum xanthocarpum i.e. asthma relieving or antihistaminic, antiallergic property. Gautam et al. (2008) studied effects of solanum xanthocarpum extract on some of the parameters likse smooth muscle relaxation, and antagonism of asthma mediators such as histamine, eiosinophils and protection against mast cell degranulation which seemed to be prominent in pathophysiology of asthma

Hepatoprotective Activity

 Polypharmaceutical herbal formulation Jigrine, containing aqueous extracts of 14 medicinal plants including solanum xanthocarpum and used for liver ailments. A. K. Najmi et al. [2005] investigated the DPPH-free radical scavenging activity, hepatoprotective and antioxidant activity of Jigrine against galactosamine induced hepatotoxicity in rats. Ant filarial effect Lalit Mohan et al. (2006)

reported the larvicidal potential of crude extracts of solanum xanthocarpum and suggested its suitability as an ecofriendl, effective larvicide in the management of mosquito populations and in limiting the outbreak of various vector borne epidemics.

Mosquito Larvicidal Effect

The plant has been used in the various fields of pest management but it is not exploited in vector control. The fruit extracts of the plant revealed larvicidal activity against An. stephensi and Cx. Quinquefasciatus and one culicine species Ae. aegypti. Volatile oil obtained from solanum xanthocarpum exhibited repellency against mosquito Cx. quinquefasciatus at a very lower concentration than those of the plants studied earlier.. The root extract is also effective against anopheline and culicine mosquito species, though at higher concentrations in comparison to fruit extract. Methanolic extract from dried fruit tissues showed antifungal activity against A. brassicae. The methanolic extract of aerial parts significantly and dose-dependently suppressed the frequency of acetic acid-induced abdominal constrictions in mice.

Summary and Conclusion

The extensive survey of literature revealed that solanum xanthocarpum is an important source of many pharmacologically and medicinally important chemicals, especially steroidal hormone solasodine and other chemicals like solasonine, campestrol, campeferol, diosgenin and various useful alkaloids. The plant is extensively studied for the various pharmacological activities like traditional antiasthmatic, antifungal activity, hepatoprotective, and mosquito repellent properties. Although the results from this review are quite promising for the use of solanum xanthocarpum as a multi-purpose medicinal agent, several limitations currently exist in the current literature. While solanum xanthocarpum has been used successfully in Ayurvedic medicine for centuries, more clinical trials should be conducted to support its therapeutic use.

References :

- Kirtikar., K.R. & Basu, B.D. (2005). Indian Medicinal Plants, (International book distributors, Vol.III,1759-1761.
- Chattergee., A. & S.C. Pakrashi (1991). The Treatise on Indian Medicinal Plants. V.I. Publication and Information Directorate, C.S.I.R. New Delhi.
- Chatterjee., A. & S.C. Pakrashi. (1995). The Treatise on Indian Medicinal Plants, V.H. Publications and Information Directorate, C.S.I.R., New Delhi.
- Chopra., R.N., L. Nayer., & I. C. Chopra (1956). Glossary of Indian Medicinal Plants. Publication and Information Directorate, C.S.I.R. New Delhi.
- Vadnere., G.P.,Gaud, R.S.& Singhai, A.K.(2008). Pharmacologyonline., 1, 513-522.
- Khare., C.P. (1995). Encyclopedia of Indian Medicinal Plants, Springer, 432-433.
- Ghani., A. (1998). Medicinal plants of Bangladesh - chemical constituents and uses. Asiatic Society of Bangladesh, Dhaka,
- Sinha., S.C. (1996). Medicinal Plants of Manipur, Mass & Sinha publications, Manipur, India,
- J. Laurila., Laakso, I., Vaananen., Kuronen, T.& Huopalahti., R. (1999). J Agric Food Chem, 47, 2738–2744.
- Trivedi., P. & Pundarikakshudu., K. (2007). Chromatographia, 65, 239-243.
- Gupta., S.Mal., M.& Bhattacharya,P. (2005).Eur Bull Drug Res, 13, 51-55.
- Sheth.,A.K. (2005). The Herbs of Ayurveda. A.K.Sheth Publisher, Vol.IV, , 1044.
- Djukanovic., R. Roche, W.R. & J.W. Wilson. (1990). Am J Respir Crit Care Med, 142, 434–457.
- Phillip., F. (2003) Mol Ther , 7, 148–152.
- Vadnere., G.P. Gaud R.S.& Singhai A.K.(2008). Pharmacologyonline, 1, 513-522. Mohan.,L. Sharma., P. & Srivastava. C.N(2006). Entomol Res, 36, 220–225.
- Mohan.,L. Sharma., P. & Srivastava. C.N. (2005). J Environ Biol, , 26(2), 399-401.
- Singh.,K.V .& Bansal., S.K.(2003). Curr Sci, 84(6), 749-751.

- Rajkumar.,S. & Jebanesan., A.(2005). Trop Biomed, 2005, 22(2), 139–142.
- Dixit., V.P. & GuptaInt., R.S. (1982) J Androl, 5(3), 295.
- Dixit., V.P(1986). J Steroid Biochem, 1986, 25, 24-27.
- Muller., J.L.& Clauson. K.A. (1997)). Am J Managed Care, 1997, 3(11), 1753-1770. 38(2), 256-260
- Gera Mohit., Gusain. Singh. Mahender., M.Y., Ansari & N.S Bishat (2005). Economics of cultivation of some commercially important medicinal plants, Indian Forester., 131(3): 358-364.
- Karam., V. & S. K. Bansal (2003). Larvisidal properties of a perennial herbs Solanum xanthocarpum against vectors of malaria and Dengu/DHF, Current Science., 84(6): 749-751.
- Nayar, C.K.N & N. Mohan (1990). Medicinal Plants of India: with special reference to Ayurveda, Nag Publishers, Delhi.
- Pundarikakshuda., K., J. K. Patel & R.K. Patel (2003). Improvement of solasodine yield from fresh berries of Solanum xanthocarpum by post harvest incubation, Journal of Medicinal and Aromatic Plant Sciences., 25(1): 66-68.
- Rai., Rajiv & Nath, Vijendra (2005). Use of medicinal plants by traditional herbal healers in Central India, Indian Forester., 131(3): 463-468.
- Najmi., A.K., Pillai, K.K., Pal, S.N.& M. Aqil. (2005) Ethnopharmacol, 97, 521–525.
- Mohan.,L .,Sharma., P.& Srivastava C.N.(2007). Southeast Asian J Trop Med Public Health,38(2), 256-260.
- Sheth,. A.K. (2005) The Herbs of Ayurveda. A.K.Sheth Publisher,Vol.IV, 1044.

Assistant Professor Botany
Govt. Nagarjuna PG College of Science Raipur C.G.
kritikajyotinamdeo@gmail.com

14. Study of landfill leachate and their Impact on the Groundwater Quality of Town Deeg District, Bharatpur (Rajasthan) India

Sunder Singh

Landfill leachate is a complicated organic wastewater generated in the sanitary landfilling process. Landfill leachate must be appropriately disposed to avoid ecotoxicity and environmental damage. An in depth understanding of the physiochemical characteristics and environmental behaviors of landfill leachate is essential for its effective treatment. Leachate and groundwater samples from different sources were collected for two sampling periods from the vicinity of dumping site within a radius of 1 km. Collected samples were analyzed for physico-chemical parameters, heavy metals. The result showed high load of organic and inorganic contaminants in leachate as it had a higher COD value (3620mgl-1 and 4523 mg l-1) whereas ammoniacal nitrogen (NH +-N) levels were 851 mg l-1 and 1296 mg l-1 for two sampling periods. The concentration of Cu and Zn were highest amongst all the analyzed heavy metals in leachate samples. Almost all parameters in groundwater samples exceeded the BIS and WHO standard limits, which showed high contamination of groundwater surrounding the dumping site. Higher concentrations of COD and NH +-N in most groundwater samples indicates percolation of landfill leachate into the groundwater aquifer, leading to its contamination. Groundwater samples collected near the dumping sites of lower depth have higher levels of pollutants than the samples collected from higher depth.

Keywords : Landfill, Leachate, Impacts on human health, Solid waste, Contamination, Groundwater.

Introduction

Landfill leachate is characterized by high chemical and biological oxygen demand and generally consists of undesirable substances such as organic and inorganic contaminants. Landfill leachate may differ depending on the content and age of landfill contents, the degradation procedure, climate and hydrological conditions. Of all available management options for solid waste management, landfill disposal is the most commonly employed waste management worldwide. Such landfill have served as ultimate waste receptors for municipal refuse, industrial or agricultural residues, wastewater sludge, incinerator ash, recycle discards, and/or treated hazardous wastes, and have thereby promoted greater interest in landfill system innovation and advancement.

In India, solid waste is disposed in an unrestricted and non-systematic way (Vijayalakshmi and Abraham, 2017), resulting in adverse ecological impacts. Improper landfill construction without an integrated impact assessment raises a severe threat to the environment as well as human health (Chaudhary et al., 2021). The major environmental problems associated with dumping sites/unsanitary landfill sites are the production of leachate and emission of greenhouse gases such as methane and carbondioxide, which is mainly attributed to high rate of waste degradation due to the presence of organic fraction. Moreover, landfill sites without bottom liners generate leachate that can enter unconfined groundwater aquifers and surface water bodies, making them unfit for various purposes, including domestic use (Fatta et al., 1999; Longe and Balogun, 2010; Gautam et al., 2011), potentially endangering the health of those living in vicinity.

The vulnerability of water sources (surface and groundwater) to leachate pollution highly depends on factors like type of dumping site, waste composition, susceptibility of an area, leachate characteristics, depth and flow of water table, etc. (Al- Khadi, 2006; Saidu, 2011; Singh et al., 2009). Additionally, its chemical properties are determined by waste composition, landfill age, oxygen availability, meteorological factors and hydrogeological conditions (Przydatek, 2021). Leachate comprised of various complex organic (degradable) and inorganic (non-degradable) compounds, including humic substances, various salts, ammoniacal nitrogen, other nitrogenous compounds, heavy metals and microbes (Kjeldsen et al., 2002; Stollenwerk and Colman, 2003; Wiszniowski et al., 2006; Mor et al., 2006). Leachate causes a threat to the surrounding environment by physical, chemical and microbiological processes due to which toxic materials transfer its pollutants to the nearby waterbodies (Naveen et al., 2017). Subsequently, these toxic pollutants during monsoon season show high percolation, disturb the groundwater table, and ultimately harm the local population living around. Additionally, the pollutants released from the landfill sites strongly affect the soil structure, which further deteriorates the growth of plants and microorganisms. Hence, landfill sites are the major sources of environmental risk due to leachate generation and its transportation through waste (Gworek et al., 2016). The effect of leachate generated from landfills on the surrounding environment had been assessed in various scientific studies (Christensen et al., 1998; Tatsi and Zouboulis, 2002; Mor et al., 2006; Rana et al., 2015, 2018; Lopezet al., 2008). In the current study, the impact of landfill leachate on the surrounding groundwater quality was investigated from the town Deeg district -Bharatpur ,Rajasthan, India. Physico-chemical parameters, heavy metals, and microbiological analysis was carried out in the collected leachate and groundwater samples to determine the potential risk to ground water quality near the dumping site. The study also examined the impact of different depths and distances of landfills from different groundwater sources (bore well and hand pump) and discussed remedial measures to prevent environmental risk. In addition, the study aimed to provide guidelines for the development and implementation of leachate treatment processes to limit the negative environmental effects.

Materials and Methods

Study area and information of dumping site: The study was conducted in town Deeg, which is spread across an area of 3 km2 Deeg a town of heritage due to historical values and world famous Jal Mahal, gardens, forts and fountains, is located at 27o28' N latitude and 77o20' E longitude with an average elevation of 174m (571 ft.) in district Bharatpur (popular for bird sanctuary– the Keoladeo Ghana National Park), Rajasthan, India. The dumping site is located near the town Deeg , Goverdhan Gate Area. This dumping site receives over 150 tonnes per day of MSW from different sources like city's residential, commercial, and institutional areas. The waste comprised 45% of organic fraction and 19% of inorganic fraction of the total generated waste of town Deeg.. Most of the recyclables or combustible fraction of waste is either picked up by the informal workers or is processed in the Refuse Derived Plant. The residential and agricultural areas are present in the vicinity of the dumping site. The population of this area is highly dependent on the groundwater for domestic and irrigation purposes.

The water is drawn through available hand pumps, government wells, or bore wells. There are several hand pumps that can be spotted around the Goverdhan Gate Area site. However, most of them are either closed by Municipal authorities due to poor water quality or are non-functional for human consumption. Keeping this in view Municipal Corporation has installed two government wells at a depth of around 320 ft. to supply water to the residents, which are located within 1 km of the dumping site. However, many functional hand pumps were observed surrounding the disposal site and groundwater samples were drawn from all available sources to assess contamination.

Collection of leachate and groundwater samples: To study the leachate percolation effect on surrounding ground water resources, the leachate and groundwater samples were collected from the adjacent areas of the dumpsite and examined for various physico-chemical parameters. Since no leachate collection facility is present near the waste dumpsite, leachate was collected randomly from leachate pools in the low-lying areas of the disposal site and around the waste piles during June-2017and June-2018. These were later methodically mixed to get a representative grab sample. Three replicates of the extract were considered for the laboratory analysis of the samples. For analysis, 14 groundwater samples were collected for two sampling periods, 1 and 2, covering a radius of 3 km from the dumping site. At the time of first sampling period, the water table depth in shallow aquifers usually ranged from 2.79 m to 3.13 m, while at the second sampling period it was reported to be 2.32 m to 2.68 m (CGWB,2016). Post collection, the samples were stored in ice-boxes and immediately transferred to laboratory for analysis.

Laboratory Analysis: Leachate and groundwater samples were stored in refrigerator at 4°C and analyzed for physico-chemical parameters following the standard methods of APHA (2012). The pH, and electrical conductivity were estimated with a pH meter and conductivity meter, respectively. Total Dissolved Solids of the samples were calculated by the United States Salinity Laboratory Staff (1954) formula. Chemical Oxygen Demand was analyzed using reflux titrimetric. Calcium, Chloride, Total Alkalinity, Carbonate, Bicarbonate, Total Hardness were analyzed by titrimetric method. Phosphate, Ammoniacal Nitrogen, Sulphate and Nitrate were analyzed by spectrophotometer while Sodium and Potassium ions were analyzed using Flame Photometry. Fluoride ion was measured by SPADNS method. Heavy metals like cadmium, chromium, copper, lead, nickel and zinc were analyzed with Atomic Absorption Spectroscopy . The MPN (Most Probable Number) method was used to estimate total coliforms by inoculating the samples in different dilutions of Mackonkey broth. After inoculation, the incubation process was carried out for 48 hrs. The total coliforms were identified by variation in the color due to the production of acid and gases in the medium. Water samples can be categorized into four classes based on counts coliform.

Statistical Analysis: The results obtained were tabulated and statistically assessed with SPSS (Statistical Package for the Social Science) package and later compared with the prescribed Standards of Bureau of Indian Standards (2012) and World Health Organization (2017). For data analysis, correlation analysis was performed in order to determine the degree of association among different variables.

Risk Assessment Conceptual Model: A robust conceptual model was developed for the risk assessment study to assess the risk of leachate percolation on the surrounding groundwater sources. The model has different stages, including historical information of the disposal site and current practices, type of solid waste dumped, monitoring of leachate and groundwater quality, evaluating risks, potential impacts, and the need for appropriate risk management measures. The present study was planned and   conducted based on these different stages.

Results and Discussion

The physico-chemical characteristics of leachate generally varies with the solid waste composition dumped and the age of the landfill

(Fatta et al., 1999; Tricys, 2002). The pH values of the leachate samples of two sampling sites were 9.36 and 6.95,indicating alkaline nature, which was due to high degradation of primary organic content producing ammonia and carbonic acid which further increases the level of pH. The pH value in leachate not only relies on the acid levels present in the leachate but also on the CO2 pressure existing in the landfill gas, which in turn contact through the leachate (Banar et al., 2006).

The leachate alkalinity reveals the age of the dumping site (Jorstad et al., 2004). This is typically noticed at landfills with disposal for last 10 years (El-Fadel et al., 2002). The alkaline pH of leachate from Town Deeg Bhartapur Rajasthan at Goverdhan Gate Area site was also discussed by Singh (2015) during pre-monsoon and post-monsoon season. In pre monsoon, the pH for three landfill sites was found to be 7.7, 7 and 6.7 while in post-monsoon the pH was as 7.13, 6.6 and 6.5. Gomes et al. (2016) demonstrated that alkaline leachate contain several toxic metals such as household batteries waste, adding toxic elements like cadmium, nickel and chromium in landfill leachate (Mor et al., 2018; Xu-Dan et al., 2015). Leachate samples were found with higher values of EC (2322and 28329 µScm-1) and TDS (17900and 19853 mg 1-1), indicating the presence of dissolved salts (Table 1)and various types of waste which is being dumped on the landfill site. High level of pH, EC and TDS were reported around the landfill sites. Amina et al. (2004) assessed the landfill leachate at Alexandria, Virginia dumpsite and reported the EC and TDS values as high as 41,637 µScm-1 and 30,083 mg 1-1, respectively. The Cl- and F- ions in the leachate samples were 2034.3 mg 1-1 and80 mg 1-1. A high NO - (159 mg 1-1) concentration was also observed in the leachate. The concentration of NH + was 2389 mg 1-1 and 5796 mg 1-1. High COD in leachate (10008 mg 1-1 and 18280 mg 1-1) indicates high amount of organic material (Kaur et al., 2016). El- Salam and Abu-Zuid (2015) reported COD values with an average of 15,629 mg 1-1. In the present study, a high concentration of NH +-N (2389 mg 1-1 and 5796 mg 1-1) was also observed in the leachate, which can be accredited to the degradation of biodegradable waste commonly due to fertilizers used in the agriculture field in the nearby areas (Mor et al., 2006). The concentration of cations was found higher than the concentration of anions. The order of cation was noticed as Ca+>Na+>K+>Mg+ whereas anions SO 2->Cl->F->PO 3-. Heavy metals (Cd, Cr, Cu, Ni, Pb and Zn) concentration was also analyzed and it was observed that Cu (4.3 ppm and 2.8 ppm) and Zn (7.01ppm and 7.1ppm) showed the highest value amongst all the studied heavy metals. Pb, Cd, Cr and Ni were found comparatively in lower concentrations indicating the disposal of hazardous wastes such as metal scraps, electronic items, medicines, paints, soiled litter, etc., at dumping site. Additionally, the high concentrations of characteristics of heavy metals at dumping areas could be due to solubility of metals (Kulikowska and Klimiuk, 2008). Groundwater around the waste dumping site is used for various domestic as well as drinking purposes. Therefore, this becomes important to analyze groundwater quality. Groundwater samples were collected within the radius of 3 km around the dumping sites. During first sampling, the pH values of collected groundwater samples ranged from 6.8 to 7.8,with an average value of 7.24. However, during second sampling, the pH values ranged from 7.2-7.7 with an average value of 7.5. As per BIS standards, the collected groundwater samples showed pH within the desirable range of 6.5-8.5. Landfill leachate may raise the pH of drinking water, resulting in the formation of trihalomethane, a poisonous chemical to humans (Kumar et al., 2010). EC values during both sampling periods were found in the range of 390 µmhos cm-1 -1861 µmhoscm-1 and 526 µmhos cm-1 - 1742 µmhos cm-1 respectively, in the samples (Fig. 2). Probably due to the presence of high level ionic species originating from nearby man made activities (Zereg et al., 2018).

Table 1: Composition of leachate collected from town Deeg , Bharatpur (Goverdhan Gate Area)

Parameters*	Sampling 1	Sampling 2
pH	9.36	6.95
EC	36982	48200
TDS	30068	34692
NH +	485	1296

NO -3	159	110
PO -4	50.14	65.5
SO4-4	1756	4322
TH	11255	6
Ca	4632.9	4996
Mg	322	511
TA	6322	9985
HCO3	6289	9986
CO3	ND	ND
COD	3620	4523
Cl	1022	1299
Na	1822	2207
K	601	635
Cr	ND	ND
Cu	4.01	2.7
Ni	ND	ND
Zn	7.06	7.12
Cd	ND	ND
Pb	0.07	0.059

* Except pH and EC, all values are in mg l-1 ND- Not Detected

TDS was noticed in the range of 249 -1191 mg l-1 and 362-1080 mg l-1 during the first and second sampling period, which was recorded higher than the WHO and BIS standards, i.e., 500 mg l-1. As per US salinity standards, groundwater samples fall under medium to high saline range category. Almost 50% of the samples resulted in high TDS values during both samplings. The high values of TDS in majority of samples indicated percolation of leachate comprising the presence of dissolved salts with high concentrations. High concentration of dissolved salts in concentration of total hardness was noticed highest (459 mg l-1) during the first and second (404 mg l-1) sampling period. According to Durfor and Beckor's (1964) classification, the collected groundwater samples fall under 'Hard' and 'Very Hard' categories. Further, Ca2+ ions ranged from 36.8-100.8 mg l-1 and 44-117mg l-1 during both sampling periods in the collected groundwater samples . Al-Sabahi et al. (2009) reported elevated levels of Ca2+ (396 mg l-1) in the groundwater samples collected from the surrounding areas of a landfill in Yemen. The Mg2+ ion concentration ranged from 10.8-50.6 mg l-1 during the first sampling period, while during the second sampling period concentration ranged from 12 -46 mg l-1, respectively. Sample S12 resulted in higher concentration of Mg2+ ions than the desirable limit of 30 mg l-1 as per BIS (2012). Total Alkalinity values in the collected samples ranged from 256-524 mg l-1 and 298-520 mg l-1 during both samplings. TA values in most samples exceeded the desirable limits of BIS (2012). The CO - hardness was not observed in groundwater samples, while HCO - hardness ranged from 294-521 mg l . It has been reported that CO2 gas produced during degradation of municipal solid waste within unlined disposal sites can be the source of high drinking water affects the palatability of water and may induce various other physiological reactions. High EC and TDS values of groundwater inferred the effect of local land fill sites and it could also be due

Table 2: Microbiological quality of groundwater near waste disposal site

S.No.	MPN	As per MaCrady's Table
S1	1/100	S
S2	3/100	S
S3	0/100	S
S4	101/100	US
S5	3/100	S
S6	35/100	US
S7	24/100	US
S8	0/100	S
S9	3/100	S
S10	3/100	S
S11	0/100	S
S12	0/100	S
S13	3/100	S
S14	0/100	S

*S:Satisfactory, US: Unsatisfacto

Urban municipal landfill leachate and 0.5 mg 1-1 in pond water and open well of Bangalore city. No guidelines for ammonia in drinking water has been given by WHO (2017), while BIS (2012) has set the acceptable level of 0.5 mg 1-1, according to which most of the samples were found above this limit. A higher level of COD (> 70 mg 1-1) in groundwater samples was found in the areas closer to dumping site. High COD content of groundwater clearly indicated the presence of organic pollutants (Mor et al., 2018; Kaur et al., 2016; Samadder, 2017). However, the concentration of COD becomes untraceable as distance increases from the dumping site . COD one of the critical components in the simulation of leachate percolation into the groundwater (Bagheri et al., 2017). Further, Na+, SO 2-, F- and PO 3-were observed well within the prescribed limits of WHO (2017) and BIS (2012). In leachate, heavy metals play an essential role in determining groundwater contamination.

The presence of heavy metals in leachate implies that it is in an intermediate stage (Mor et al., 2018). Among various heavy metals analyzed in the groundwater samples, Cd and Cr were found below detectable limit. However, Cu content was found above the desirable limit in most samples ranging from 0-0.14 ppm during both sampling periods . Cu content in also found above the desirable limit of 0.05 ppm in most groundwater samples. The average value of Pb in all groundwater samples varied from 0.05-0.18 ppm and 0.06-0.18 ppm . The concentration of Zn was reported to be higher. Still, it was well within the acceptable limit of 5 ppm, which may be due to Zn containing waste such as fertilizers, automobiles, industrial effluent and landfill leachate (Singh et al., 2008; Kurakalva et al., 2016; Choudhury et al., 2021). As shown in Fig. 5, the Zn content in groundwater samples ranged from 0-0.81 ppm and BDL-0.083 ppm. In previous studies, Boateng et al. (2019) reported high level of Pb, Fe, and Cd in well water due to landfill percolation. Similarly, Vongdala et al. (2019) reported high levels of heavy metals in groundwater samples that bordered municipal solid waste. Indicating leaching out of heavy metals from the landfill waste, total coliforms were tested in groundwater samples following the MPN groundwater can be from the leaching effect of dumping sites (Kanmani and Gandhimathi, 2013).The concentration of Pb was method. Out of 14 sampling locations, three sites S4, S6 and S7 showed the presence of coliforms in groundwater samples (Table 2). S4 and S6 samples were in close vicinity of the dumping site where handpump depth was shallow (25ft.). The presence of coliforms in groundwater samples again confirm leachate percolation to shallow aquifers releasing poisonous compounds that contaminate water sources (Kaushik et al., 2018).

Table 3: Variation in chemical parameters concerning the age of various groundwater extraction

Parameters	1-5 years	5-15 years	20-30 years
COD	24.9	11.16	56.2
NH+	0.219	0.66	0.58
Cl-	43.96	64.52	18.17

Sources : (Handpumps, Tube wells and Submersible pumps).

The results were found coherent with previously conducted studies (Chetna et al., 2006; Malan et al., 2020). The extent of groundwater contamination with leachate percolation is influenced by numerous factors such as leachate composition, contiguity of water source, age and depth of groundwater sources, etc. In this study, the degree of contamination of groundwater sources was related to the age, distance and depth of the source by taking key parameters like NH +, K+, Cl-, COD into consideration which are the main tracer of contamination through leachate. Tables 4 and 5 shows variation in different species concentrations at different depths. It was noticed that a high level of COD was fount at lowest depth of $0 - 30$ ft whereas at 30-60 ft. and 60-90 ft, high concentrations of NH +, K+, Cl- ions clearly showed leachate infiltration into the aquifer. In addition, the concentration of these species decreased as depth increased due dilution of leachate . Comparable results have been reported by Naveen et al. (2017) for MSW landfill at Karnatka and Mor et al. (2018) for the dumping site of Jalandhar, Punjab. Based on the results, it can be concluded that leachate percolation significantly contaminates groundwater sources close to dumping site at lower depth. An attempt was also made to study the effect of age on water quality. High contamination was reported in old hand pumps/ submersibles/ supply wells. Sampling revealed a higher range of COD, K+, Cl- and NH + in the samples that were collected from older pumps/wells, i.e., 20-30 years and 5-15 years old, showing that the aquifer was affected by the percolation of leachate as the age of dumpsite was also 29 years old. It has been observed that a close relationship exists in pollutant contamination with distance, depth and age of water source due to the well developed methanogenic conditions. This also showed the variation in the concentration of ionic species and inorganic pollutants. As the depth increases the concentration of ionic species decreases and concentration of inorganic pollutants increases. The study results were found coherent to the previously conducted studies. Correlation analysis was used to estimate the relationship amongst different variables. A positive correlation coefficient (r) indicates that the level of individual variable increases with the increase in the level of other variables and vice versa. In contrast, a negative correlation indicates that the level of individual variable increases with decrease in the level of other variables. The observations of correlation analysis suggest that some parameters have a reasonable correlation with each other, indicating their close association. It was observed that EC is significantly correlated with TDS (0.984**) and K+ (0.578**) at a significant level of 0.01 and 0.05, respectively. TDS was found to have a strong positive correlation with NO - and K+. NO - was found to be significantly and positively correlated with TH (0.761**) and Mg2+ (0.745**) at a significant level of 0.01, while K+ was reported to be positively correlated to EC, TDS, TH and Mg2+. TH was also found to be highly associated with Ca2+, Mg2+, K+, SO 2-, PO 3-, and Cl-, which showed the exact source of pollutants. Further, Na+ was found positively correlated to TA (0.773**) while K+ was reported to be positively correlated to EC, TDS, TH and Mg2+. COD was found negatively correlated to Ca2+ (-0.634*), TA (- 0.651*) and K+ (-0.550*) at a significance level of 0.05. The results of the correlation analysis were found coherent with the previously conducted studies (Mor et al., 2006; Srivastava et al., 2008; Aboyeji et al., 2016; Negi et al., 2020).

Overall, the study results indicated that the aquifer is not suitable for domestic use for the population living in the proximity of Dadumajra dumpsite. The exceedingly high levels of physico-chemical parameters including Total Coliforms and heavy metals in the groundwater samples, indicate significant threat to the health of the consumers. In addition, the level of contamination in groundwater sources owing to the percolation of leachate directly correlates with factors like depth, distance, and age of water sources. Therefore, the findings of this study confirm that the unscientific disposal site located in town Deeg , Goverdhan Gate Area, poses a threat to the surrounding groundwater resources. Hence, there is a need to take immediate remedial measures such as (i) closing the existing dumpsite, as it has already reached its capacity; (ii) converting unscientific dumpsite into sanitary landfill with the provision of leachate collection and treatment system; (iii) if sufficient funds are available with the municipality, remediation of the site and aquifer can be done; (iv) sanitary landfill site should be constructed and made in operation with a provision of leachate collection and treatment facility; to prevent further infiltration of leachate into the groundwater.

There is an urgent need to formulate a corrective action plan that aims to prevent further contamination of the aquifer and prevent leachate percolation. Some of the possible options to avoid risks associated with the contaminated site and ensure suitable water quality may include (I) closing the existing dumpsite, as it has already reached its capacity; (ii) converting unscientific dumpsite into sanitary landfill with the provision of leachate collection and treatment system; (iii) close all the hand pumps and tube wells in the close proximity of the dumping site, even those located at deeper depth, as there are possible chances of contamination; (iv) if sufficient funds are available with the municipality, remediation of the site and aquifer can be done; (v) sanitary landfill site should be constructed and made in operation with a provision of leachate collection and treatment facility.

References

Aboyeji, O.S. and S.F. Eigbokhan: Evaluations of groundwater contamination by leachates around Olusosun open dumpsite in Lagos metropolis, Southwest Nigeria. J. Environ. Manage., 183, 333–341 (2016).

Akinbile, C.O. and M.S. Yusoff: Environmental impact of leachate pollution on groundwater supplies in Akure, Nigeria. Int. J. Environ. Sci. Dev., 2, 81-86 (2011).

Al-Sabahi, E., A. Rahim, W.Y. Zuhairi, F. Al-Nozaily and F.Al-Shaebi: The characteristics of leachate and groundwater pollution at the municipal solid waste landfill of Ibb city, Yemen. Am. J. Environ. Sci., 5, 256-266 (2009).

Amina, C., Y. Abdekader, L. Elkbri, M. Jacky and V. Alain: Environmental impact of an urban landfill on a coastal aquifer (El-Jadida, Morocco). J. African Earth Sci., 39, 509-516 (2004).

APHA: Standard Methods for Examination of Water and Wastewater.19thEdn., APHA, AWWA, WPCF, Washington DC, USA(2012).

Bagheri, M., A. Bazvand and M. Ehteshami: Application of artificial intelligence for the management of landfill leachate penetration into groundwater, and assessment of its environmental impacts. J. Clean. Prod., 149, 784-796 (2017).

Banar, M., O. Aysun and K. Mine: Characterization of the leachate in an urban landfill by physicochemical analysis and solid phase micro- extraction. GC/MS. Environ. Monit. Assess., 121, 439-459 (2006).

Bhalla, G., P.K. Swamee, A. Kumar and A. Bansal: Assessment of groundwater quality near municipal solid waste landfill by an Aggregate Index Method. Int. J. Environ. Sci., 2, 1492-1503 (2012).

BIS: Bureau of Indian Standads-Indian Standards Specification for Drinking Water IS: 10500, New Delhi (2012).

Boateng, T.K., F. Opoku, S.O. Acquaah and O. Akoto: Pollution evaluation, sources and risk assessment of heavy metals in hand-dug wells from Ejisu-Juaben Municipality, Ghana. Environ. Syst. Res., 4, 18 (2015).

Castaneda, S.S., R.J. Sucgang, R.V. Almoneda, N.D.S. Mendoza and C.P.C. David: Environmental isotopes and major ions for tracing leachate contamination from a municipal landfill in Metro Manila, Philippines. J. Environ. Radioact., 110, 30-37 (2012).

CGWB: Central Ground Water Board Report, Water Quality Issues and Challenges in Punjab (2016).

Chaudhary, R., P. Nain and A. Kumar: Temporal variation of leachate pollution index of Indian landfill sites and associated human health risk. Environ. Sci. Pollut. Res., 28, 28391-28406 (2021).

Chetna, A., A. Pratima and C. Rina: Bacteriological water quality status of River Yamuna in Delhi. J. Environ. Biol., 27, 97-101(2006).

Choudhury, M., D.S. Jyethi, J. Dutta, S.P. Purkayastha, D. Deb, R. Das,

G. Roy, T. Sen and K.G. Bhattacharyya: Investigation of groundwater and soil quality near to a municipal waste disposal site in Silchar, Assam, India. Int. J. Energy Water Resour., 4, 1-11 (2021).

Christensen, J.B., D.L. Jensen, Z. Filip, C. Gron, F. Zdenek and T.H Christensen: Characterization of the dissolved organic carbon in landfill polluted groundwater. Water Resour., 32, 125-135 (1998).

Durfor, C. N. and E. Becker: Public water supplies of the 100 largest cities in the US; US-Geo. Survey water Paper,1812, 364 pages (1964).

El-Fadel, M., E. Bou-Zeid, W. Chahine and B. Alayli: Temporal variation of leachate quality from pre-sorted and baled municipal solid waste with high organic and moisture content. Waste Manage., 22, 269–282 (2002).

El-Salam, M.M.A. and G. I. Abu-Zuid: Impact of landfill leachate on the groundwater quality: A case study in Egypt. J. Adv. Res., 6, 579–586 (2015).

Fatta, D., A. Papadopoulos and M. Loizidou: A study on the landfill leachate and its impact on the groundwater quality of the greater area. Environ. Geochem. Hlth., 21, 175–190 (1999).

Gautam, A., G. Pathak and A. Sahni: Assessment of ground water quality at municipal solid waste dumping site-sewapura, Jaipur. Curr. World Environ., 6, 279-282 (2011).

Gomes, P., T. Valente, M.A.S. Braga, J.A. Grande and M.L. De la Torre: Enrichment of trace elements in the clay size fraction of mining soils. Environ. Sci. Pollut. Res., 23, 6039-6045 (2016).

Gworek, B., W. Dmuchowski, E. Koda, M. Marecka, A. Baczewska, P. Brągoszewska, A. Sieczka and P. Osinski: Impact of the municipal solid waste łubna landfill on environmental pollution by heavy metals. Water, 8, 470 (2016).

Jorstad, L.B, J. Jankowski and R.I. Acworth: Analysis of the distribution of inorganic constituents in a landfill leachate contaminated aquifers Astrolabe Park, Sydney, Australia. Environ. Geol., 46, 263–272 (2004).

Kanmani, S. and R. Gandhimathi: Investigation of physicochemical characteristics and heavy metal distribution profile in groundwater system around the open dump site. Appl. Water Sci., 3, 387–399 (2013).

Kaur, K., S. Mor and K. Ravindra: Removal of chemical oxygen demand from landfill leachate using cow-dung ash as a low-cost adsorbent.
J. Colloid Interf. Sci., 469, 338-343 (2016).

Kaushik, M., A.V. Nandi and V.B. Mungurwadi: Portable sensors for water pathogens Detection Mater. Today Proc., 5, 10821-10826 (2018).

Kjeldsen, I.P., M.A. Barlaz, A.P. Rooker, A. Baun, A. Ledin and T.H. Christensen: Present and long-term composition of MSW landfill leachate: A review. Criti. Rev. Environ. Sci. Technol., 32, 297-336 (2002).

Kulikowska, D. and E. Klimiuk: The effect of landfill age on municipal leachate composition. Bioresour. Technol., 99, 5981–5985 (2008).

Kumar, A., B. Bisht, V. Joshi, A.K. Singh and A. Talwar: Physical, chemical andbacteriological study of water from
rivers of Uttarakhand. J.Hum. Ecol., 32, 169-173 (2010).

Kurakalva, R.M., K.K. Aradhi, K.Y. Mallela and S. Venkatayogi: Assessment of groundwater quality in and around the Jawaharnagar municipal solid waste dumping site at Greater Hyderabad, Southern India. Procedia. Environ. Scien., 35, 328- 336 (2016).

Longe, E.O. and M.R. Balogun: Groundwater quality assessment near a municipal landfill, Lagos, Nigeria. Res. J. Appl. Sci. Eng. Technol., 2, 39–44 (2010).

Lopez, A.R., J.R. Hernandez, O.L. Mancilla, C.C. Diazconti and M.M.L. Garrido: Assessment of groundwater contamination by landfill leachate: Acase in México. Waste Manage., 28, 33–39 (2008).

Malan, A., V. Kumar and H.R. Sharma: Bacteriological evaluation of groundwater in open-defecation-free villages of Kurukshetra district, Haryana, India. Int. J. Environ. Sci., 77, 928-941(2020).

Mor, S., K. Kaur and K. Ravindra: SWOT Analysis of waste management practices in Chandigarh, India and prospects for sustainable cities, J. Environ. Biol., 37, 327-332 (2015).

Mor, S., K. Ravindra, R.P. Dahiya and A. Chandra: Leachate characterization and assessment of groundwater pollution near municipal solid waste landfill site. Environ. Monit. Assess., 118, 435-456 (2006).

Mor, S., P. Negi and R. Khaiwal: Assessment of groundwater pollution by landfills in India using leachate pollution index and estimation of error. Environ. Nanotechnol. Monit. Manag., 10, 467-476 (2018).

Naveen, B.P., D.M. Mahaparta, T.G. Sitharam, P.V. Sivapullaiah and T.V. Ramachandra: Physico-chemical and biological characterization of urban municipal landfill leachate. Environ. Pollut., 220,1–12 (2017).

Negi, P., S. Mor and K. Ravindra: Impact of landfill leachate on the groundwater quality in three cities of North India and health risk assessment. Environ. Dev. Sustain., 22, 1455-1474 (2020).

Pan, C., K. T. W. Ng, and A. Richter: An integrated multivariate statistical approach for the evaluation of spatial variations in groundwater quality near an unlined landfill. Environ. Sci. Pollut. Res., 26, 5724- 5737(2019).

Przydatek, G. and W. Kanownik: Physicochemical indicators of the influence of a lined municipal landfill on groundwater quality: A case study from Poland. Environ. Earth Sci., 80, 1-14 (2021).

Raju, N. J., P. Ram and S. Dey: Groundwater quality in the lower Varuna river basin, Varanasi district, Uttar Pradesh. J. Geol. Soc. India, 73, 178-192 (2009).

Rana, R., R. Ganguly and A.K. Gupta: An assessment of solid waste management system in Chandigarh city, India. Electron. J. Geotech. Eng., 20, 1547-1572 (2015).

Rana, R., R. Ganguly and A.K. Gupta: Indexing method for assessment of pollution potential of leachate from non-engineered landfill sites and its effect on ground water quality. Environ. Monit. Assess., 190, 46 (2018).

Ravindra, K., K. Kaur and S. Mor: System analysis of municipal solid waste management in Chandigarh and minimization practices for cleaner emissions. J. Clean. Prod., 89, 251-256 (2015).

Saidu, M.: Effect of refuse dumps on ground water quality. Adv. Appl. Sci.

Res., 2, 595-599 (2011).

Samadder, S.R., R. Prabhakar, D. Khan, D. Kishan and M.S. Chauhan: Analysis of the contaminants released from municipal solid waste landfill site: A case study. Sci. Total Environ., 580, 593–601(2017).

Singh, R.K., M. Datta, and A.K. Nema: A new system for groundwater contamination hazard rating of   landfills. J. Environ. Manage., 91, 344-357 (2009).

Singh S.: Impact of solid waste effect on ground water and soil quality in town Deeg (Bharatpur)Rajasthan. J. Asian Reson.,-4, 99-107(2015).

Singh, U.K., M. Kumar, R. Chauhan, P.K. Jha, A.L. Ramanathan and V. Subramanian: Assessment of the impact of landfill on groundwater quality: A case study of the Pirana site in western India. Environ. Monit. Assess., 141, 309-321 (2008).

Srivastava, S.K., and A.L. Ramanathan: Geochemical assessment of groundwater quality in vicinity of Bhalswa landfill, Delhi, India, using graphical and multivariate statistical methods. J. Environ. Geol., 53, 1509–1528 (2008).

Stollenwerk, K.G. and J.A. Colman: Natural remediation potential of arsenic contaminated groundwater in Welch; Arsenic in groundwater- Geochem and Occurrence, pp. 351-379 (2003).

Tatsi, A.A. and A.I. Zouboulis: A field investigation of the quantity and quality of leachate from a municipal solid waste landfill in a mediterranean climate (Thessaloniki, Greece), Adv. Environ. Res., 6, 207-219 (2002).

Tricys, V.: Research of leachate, surface and ground water pollution near Siauliai landfill, Environ. Res. Eng. Manage., 19, 30-33 (2002).

Vijayalakshmi, P. and M. Abraham: Adverse effects of physicochemical parameters of solid waste disposal on ground water quality-A case study. Res. J. Pharm., Biol. Chem., 8, 151-163 (2017).

Vongdala, N., H.D. Tran, T.D. Xuan, R. Teschke and T. Khanh: Heavy metal accumulation in water, soil, and plants of municipal solid waste landfill in Vientiane, Laos. Int. J. Environ. Res. Public Hlth., 16, 22 (2019).

WHO & UNICEF: Progress on Drinking Water, Sanitation and Hygiene: Update and SDG Baselines. Licence, Geneva (2017).

Wiszniowski, J., D. Robert, J. Surmacz-Gorska, K. Miksch and J.V. Weber: Landfill leachate treatment methods: A review. Environ. Chem. Lett., 4, 51–61 (2006).

Xu-dan, Z., Z. Chun-li, Q. Tong-bao, W. Ying, G. Tai-jun and S. Xiao- gang: Characteristics and evaluation on heavy metal contamination in Changchun municipal waste landfill after closure. J. Environ. Biol., 36, 857 (2015).

Zereg, S., A. Boudoukha and L. Benaabidate: Impacts of natural conditions and anthropogenic activities on groundwater quality in Tebessa plain, Algeria Sustain. Environ. Res., 28, 340-349

Associate Professor
Department of Zoology (Hydrotoxicology lab)
M.S.J. Govt. (P.G.) College, Bharatpur,
Rajasthan, India
email : sunderbtp@gmail.com

15. Reflection of Cultural Harmony in the Literary Works of Sultan Bahu with Special Reference to Abyat E Bahu

Prof.Dr.Rajani Shivajirao Patil*

Lect.Peerzada Sadique Ali Nishat Ali**

Abstract

This research focuses on the topic of "*Reflection of Cultural Harmony* in the Literary Works of Sultan Bahu with Special Reference to Abyat E Bahu." which reflects a universal message of tolerance and forgiveness and countering the social evils such as radicalization, extremism, and greediness which are the root causes of all social evil. Sufi Literature spreads the message of peace and harmony in society. Sultan Bahu was a Sufi poet who lived in the 17th century. His poetry, particularly his collection known as Abyat-e-Bahu, offers a rich reflection of cultural harmony. Bahu's poetry emphasizes the importance of recognizing the common humanity that unites all people, regardless of their cultural or religious background His work is considered a valuable contribution to Sufi literature, which emphasizes the importance of spiritual connection and mysticism. Through his poetry, Bahu encourages readers to focus on inner spiritual growth and development, rather than material possessions or outward appearances. His work has been an inspiration to many people throughout history and continues to be widely read and studied today. He celebrates the beauty of diversity and calls for mutual respect and tolerance among people of different faiths and beliefs. Through his poetry, Bahu provides a powerful example of the role that literature can play in promoting cultural harmony and understanding. This study provides an overview of the key themes and insights that emerge from the literary works of Sultan Bahu, with a particular focus on Abyat-e-Bahu.

Keywords : Sufi Literature, Harmony, Conflicts, Reflection, Cultural harmony, Sufi poetry, Mystical poetry, Islamic spirituality, Literary works

Introduction

In Shorkot in Jhang, Sultan Bahoo was born in 1629. His pious mother raised him after his father passed away as a child. His higher tiers of transcendence developed under his mother's maternal care and spiritual guidance, a Sufi herself. She named him Bahoo after observing him go through a euphoric phase. Ba means "with," and Hoo stands for Allah (the Almighty).

Sufism has contributed significantly to the development of literature over the years, and it is also connected to the magnificent literary achievements of Islam during its golden period, which lasted from the seventh to the thirteenth century. Sufi literature first appeared. After that, this literature flourished for centuries, covering a wide range of subjects: mystical poetry, anecdotes, manuals, metaphysics, and treatises on Islamic philosophy and religion. For novices, Sufi manuals were produced. They acted as a code of conduct and a lighthouse for their appropriate actions and procedures. The pupils were also instructed to maintain a close bond with their teacher, concentrate intently during meditation, and show piety and devotion to God.

The literary works of Sultan Bahu, a prominent Sufi poet and spiritual figure of South Asia, are recognized for their profound reflection of the cultural harmony prevalent in the region. His poetry and writings have been a significant source of inspiration and guidance for many, both in his time and today. Among his works, Abyat E Bahu stands out as a remarkable collection of mystical poetry that delves deep into the themes of Islamic spirituality, divine love, and the human condition. In this paper, we will explore the ways in which Sultan Bahu's literary works reflect the cultural harmony of South Asia, with a particular focus on *Abyat E Bahu*. By examining the language, themes, and motifs present in his poetry, we hope to gain a deeper understanding of the cultural and spiritual milieu that influenced Sultan Bahu's writing, and the relevance of his works for contemporary readers.

 Information is widely disseminated and easier to access in the modern day. Globalization has a significant impact on regional thinking, which is changing how people interpret politics, literature, and culture. The world's nations are getting more and more varied, and this trend will likely continue soon. The twenty-first century is when various civilizations interact with one another, and there are many different viewpoints available to us. As a result, we must see a range of economic, social, political, and intellectual concerns from a global perspective. Sufi literature is not limited to a single country or area in the era of globalization. The lyrical philosophy of the Sufis depicts a society's deeply ingrained culture.

Sultan Bahu was a 17th-century Sufi poet and saint who lived in what is now Pakistan. His literary works have had a profound impact on the culture and spirituality of South Asia, particularly in the regions of Punjab and Sindh. Sultan Bahu's poetry is characterized by its profound mysticism, spiritual depth, and unique literary style. His works are renowned for their ability to convey complex spiritual concepts and ideas in a simple and accessible manner.

One of Sultan Bahu's most celebrated works is *Abyat E Bahu*, a collection of his mystical poetry that has been translated into multiple languages and remains popular among readers and scholars alike. *Abyat E Bahu* consists of a series of quatrains or **"rubais"** that explore the themes of divine love, spiritual enlightenment, and the human condition. The language used in *Abyat E Bahu* is a combination of classical and colloquial Punjabi, which gives the poetry a unique flavor and makes it accessible to a wide range of readers.

The cultural harmony reflected in Sultan Bahu's poetry can be attributed to his deep understanding of the cultural and spiritual landscape of South Asia. Sultan Bahu was a devout Muslim and follower of the Sufi tradition, which emphasizes the importance of spiritual experience and personal transformation. Sufism has played a significant role in shaping the culture and spirituality of South Asia, and its influence is evident in Sultan Bahu's poetry.

Furthermore, Sultan Bahu's poetry reflects the cultural diversity of South Asia, particularly in the context of his native region of Punjab. The language and themes used in his poetry draw on a rich and diverse cultural heritage that includes Islamic, Hindu, Sikh, and folk traditions. This diversity is reflected in the language and motifs present in his poetry, which are a blend of classical Persian, Arabic, and Punjabi, as well as local dialects and idioms.

Sultan Bahu's literary works, particularly Abyat E Bahu, are a testament to the cultural and spiritual harmony that exists in South Asia. His poetry reflects the richness and diversity of the region's cultural heritage and highlights the universal themes of love, compassion, and spiritual enlightenment that transcend cultural and linguistic boundaries. Sultan Bahu's works continue to inspire readers and scholars around the world, and their relevance and significance remain undiminished even today.

Cultural Harmony and *Peace* in the works of *Sultan Bahu*

The message of Sultan Bahoo applies to everyone, regardless of caste, religion, or ethnicity. In his prose and poetry, he discusses topics like Faqr, meditation, austerity, self-actualization, and similar issues relevant to everyone. Sultan Bahoo invites us to take a holistic view of this world. Because transient material ambitions, like the quest for wealth and power, invariably result in chaos and conflicts.

The big problem in our time is that life has become superficial, and people want to show off their wealth. I want to be rich. Likewise, nations want dominance over others even if they have to exploit them. Sultan Bahu warns against this attitude which leads to the devastation of all mankind.

Wish to live like dead, then adopt a lifestyle of Faqeers (Mystics) - Hoo,
If rubbish thrown at you then endure it - Hoo,
If someone abuses or shouts at you, be polite to him - Hoo,
Tolerate noise, taunts, insult and humiliation for the sake of Friend - Hoo,
The most powerful holds our reins Bahoo, live as He makes you live - Hoo.

Sultan Bahoo believed that most social, racial, linguistic, regional and societal problems would end when all members of society recognize that God's reality is closest to the core of man. With such confidence, false vanity, pride, and a sense of superiority can be eradicated from society at the national and international levels. People's selfish approach is the root cause of all cultural, social and regional conflicts. Sultan Bahoo's concept of self-awareness is the key to resolving these conflicts. When each person discovers the one reality of his soul, internal conflicts diminish, and rays of harmony and reconciliation emanate from him. The Sufi message was so powerful that diverse societies in the country could observe peace.

Review of Literature :

The literature on the reflection of cultural harmony in the literary works of Sultan Bahu, particularly with reference to *Abyat E Bahu*, is a rich and diverse body of scholarship. Scholars have examined various aspects of Sultan Bahu's poetry, including its language, themes, motifs, and cultural context, to gain a deeper understanding of its significance and relevance. One of the prominent themes that emerges from the literature is the importance of language in Sultan Bahu's poetry. Scholars have noted that Sultan Bahu's poetry is a unique blend of classical and colloquial Punjabi, which makes it accessible to a wide range of readers. Moreover, the language used in his poetry reflects the cultural diversity of South Asia, particularly in the context of Punjab, where multiple languages and dialects are spoken. Scholars have noted that this diversity is reflected in the language and motifs used in his poetry, which draw on a rich and diverse cultural heritage that includes Islamic, Hindu, Sikh, and folk traditions.

Another significant theme that emerges from the literature is the spiritual and mystical dimension of Sultan Bahu's poetry. Scholars have noted that Sultan Bahu was a prominent figure in the Sufi tradition, which emphasizes the importance of spiritual experience and personal transformation. His poetry reflects this tradition, as it explores the themes of divine love, spiritual enlightenment, and the human condition. Scholars have noted that Sultan Bahu's poetry is not only a source of spiritual guidance for readers but also a reflection of the cultural and spiritual landscape of South Asia.

Furthermore, the literature on Sultan Bahu's poetry highlights the relevance and significance of his works for contemporary readers. Sultan Bahu's poetry continues to inspire readers around the world and remains a source of guidance and inspiration for those seeking spiritual enlightenment. Moreover, his works have been translated into multiple languages, which has helped to make them accessible to a wider audience. The literature on the reflection of cultural harmony in the literary works of Sultan Bahu is a rich and diverse body of scholarship that highlights the significance and relevance of his poetry. Scholars have explored various aspects of his poetry, including its language, themes, and cultural context, to gain a deeper understanding of its significance and relevance. The literature on Sultan Bahu's poetry reflects the universal themes of love, compassion, and spiritual enlightenment, which continue to resonate with readers today.

Sultan Bahu's literary works, particularly *Abyat E Bahu*, are renowned for their poetic beauty, profound mysticism, and reflection of the cultural harmony prevalent in South Asia. In addition to the themes and motifs discussed earlier, Sultan Bahu's poetry is also characterized by its use of literary devices and imagery. Here are a few examples:

Simile : "The heart is like a bird in a cage, waiting to be set free." This simile reflects Sultan Bahu's belief that the human heart is the seat of the soul and must be liberated from worldly desires to attain spiritual enlightenment.

Metaphor : "Love is a river that flows endlessly." This metaphor conveys the idea that divine love is a never-ending source of spiritual nourishment and enlightenment.

Personification : "The night is weeping, and the stars are shining in sympathy." This personification reflects Sultan Bahu's belief in the interconnectedness of all things and the notion that even inanimate objects can display emotions.

Symbolism : "The rose is a symbol of love, and the thorn is a symbol of sacrifice." This symbolism reflects the Sufi belief that spiritual enlightenment requires sacrifice and the willingness to endure hardship and pain.

Imagery : "The moon rises like a silver disk, casting its soft glow over the world." This imagery conveys the beauty and majesty of nature and reflects Sultan Bahu's belief in the interconnectedness of all things.

These literary devices and imagery are just a few examples of the rich and diverse poetic language that Sultan Bahu employs in his works. They contribute to the beauty and power of his poetry and help to convey the timeless themes of love, compassion, and spiritual enlightenment that continue to inspire readers today.

Conclusion :

In conclusion, the literary works of Sultan Bahu, particularly his collection of poetry known as Abyat-e-Bahu, offer a rich reflection of cultural harmony. His poetry reflects a deep understanding and appreciation of the cultural diversity that existed in the region at the time, as well as a commitment to promoting harmony and understanding among people of different cultures and religions. Through his poetry, Bahu offers a powerful message of unity and compassion, reminding readers of the common bonds that connect all people. His work is a testament to the fact that literature can be a powerful tool for promoting understanding and tolerance, and can help to overcome the barriers that divide us. Through his poetry, Bahu emphasizes the importance of recognizing the common humanity that unites all people, regardless of their cultural or religious background. He celebrates the beauty of diversity and calls for mutual respect and tolerance among people of different faiths and beliefs. His poetry remains a source of inspiration and insight for people around the world who are seeking to build bridges of understanding across cultural and religious divides. The study of Sultan Bahu's poetry can help to promote cultural harmony and understanding, particularly among young people. By introducing students to Bahu's work, educators can encourage them to think critically about issues related to diversity and inclusion, and to develop a deeper appreciation for the cultural and religious heritage of the Indian subcontinent. By promoting the study of literature that promotes peace and harmony, we can help to build a more peaceful and harmonious world for future generations.

Work Cited :

➢ Ahmed, S. (2014). Reflection of Cultural Harmony in the Poetry of Sultan Bahu. International Journal of Humanities and Social Science Research, 3(1), 1-12.

➢ Bukhari, G. A. (2009). The Poetry of Sultan Bahu: A Study in Mysticism. Islamic Studies, 48(2), 211-224.

- Farooqi, I. A. (2010). The Poetry of Sultan Bahu and its Relevance to Contemporary Society. International Journal of Humanities and Social Science, 1(3), 88-95.
- Jafri, M. A. (2017). Sultan Bahu: His Life, Works, and Message. Journal of Islamic Thought and Civilization, 7(1), 101-114.
- Khursheed, A. (2013). The Language of Poetry of Sultan Bahu: A Socio-Cultural Study. Language in India, 13(4), 249-256.
- M. A. Rahbeen, Comparative Study of Haḍrat Sultan Bahoo. in International Haḍrat Sultan *Bahoo* Conference, Islamabad: MUSLIM Institute, 2013.
- Malik, M. S. (2018). Reflection of Cultural Harmony in Sultan Bahu's Poetry. Journal of Humanities and Social Sciences, 23(2), 113-126.
- Mirza, N. A. (2011). Sultan Bahu's Poetry and its Relevance to Contemporary Society. Islamic Studies, 50(4), 599-616.
- N. A. Nomani, The general acceptance and spiritual inspiration of Sultan Bahu poetry, The Islamic culture, 2019.
- S. Bahoo, Nūr-ul-Hudā. Tr. by M.A. Khan. Lahore: Arifeen Publications, 2019.
- Sarwar, G. (2015). Sufi Philosophy and its Relevance to Contemporary Society with Reference to the Poetry of Sultan Bahu. Bulletin of Education and Research, 37(2), 187-200.
- T. Sarwar, Sultan Bahoo, 2011. Retrieved from https://www.sultanbahoo.net/blog/transforming-message-from-the-teachings-of-hazrat-sakhi-sultan-bahoo-ra

*Professor
Loknete Vyankatrao Hiray Arts Science and Commerce
College, Nashik, Maharashtra
email : rajanispatil9@gmail.com
**Lecturer
Loknete Vyankatrao Hiray Arts Science and Commerce
College, Nashik, Maharashtra
email : sadiqueali92@gmail.com

16. Environment and Education

Asheera Banu Sangli

Abstract

Environment is very important for all the living being. Creating awareness about the environment amongst the teachers and the students in educational institute is a must. Lot of opportunities are being created to study about environment from primary school to postdoctoral study, Many schools and colleges have National service scheme, Rovers and Rangers, National cadet corps and many number of environmental clubs wherein students and teachers can take part. They can also create awareness to public regarding the environment and sustainable development, Environment studies is one of the compulsory subject offered for primary to under graduate students in India. Different branches of studies related to environmental studies are toxicology, environmental disasters, aquatic biology, pollution studies, pollution law, agriculture sciences, biotechnology, microbiology, botany, zoology, chemistry, physics, mathematics , statistics, wild life conservation, energy conservation, birding and many more. Projects are undertaken by students and teachers based on the interested environmental themes, The teachers and the students should understand how important the environment is for the future and incorporate in their daily life as well.

Keywords : Environment, Education, Teachers, Students.

Introduction

Environment consists of biotic and abiotic factors and are interrelated. Human has been understanding and is gaining more knowledge about the environment. Different streams of science, arts or commerce has contributed more to understand environment and make use of environment in a sustainable way. For the sustainable development and conservation of natural resources, environmental education plays an important role. Scientific studies helped us in understanding universe, planets, earth, rain, weather patterns, nature's natural cycles like hydrological cycle, carbon cycle, lithosphere, atmosphere and various knowledge of environment. Teachers play an important role in making the students to understand and create awareness about the environment.

Creating Awareness about Environment

Teacher can create awareness about environment at any age students, addressing them by keeping themselves and their surrounding clean and tidy. Creating interest in the students about the biotic and abiotic factors surrounding them, caring for them .and make the students to have eco friendly habits like not spitting, no smoking, reduce the use of plastics, creating zero pollution zone in the campus, creating awareness amongst girl students about their personal hygiene. toilet habits.

Knowledge about Environment

It is duty of the teacher to gain knowledge and give knowledge about the environment by classroom teaching or online teaching through various websites, information or computer based knowledge and using various reference books. Environment studies is one of the compulsory subject offered for primary to under graduate students in India. Different branches of studies related to environment are taught, like toxicology, environmental disasters, aquatic biology, pollution studies, pollution law, agriculture sciences, biotechnology, microbiology, botany, zoology, chemistry, physics, mathematics, statistics, wild life conservation, energy conservation, birding and many more. Getting knowledge from experts. Teaching about Sustainable Development Goals. and make students to do review of literature The teachers and students can make use of SWAYAM, IGNOU, Coursera and many other platforms to upgrade themselves in various fields of environment.

Motivating Students about Environment

Motivating the students about the different current environmental issues like pollution, toxicology, ecology, limnology, aquatic biology, soil biology, atmospheric studies, climate change and to take up active participation in projects related to solid waste management, reduction of carbon, climate change, use of environment friendly nonconventional resources..

Skill Development

Various fields of environmental studies require laboratory or field work and teacher can teach the students the skills to handle the various issues of environment by performing experiments, bioassays, keen observation, different laboratory techniques, handing of equipment, handling and caring for experimental animals, observational studies in the field, behavior of the animals, create modules and patent modelling.

Research and Critical Thinking

Various research can be taken by the teachers involving students and enhance their critical thinking and solving the problems to have a sustainable environment. Projects are undertaken by teachers and students, In Karnataka state universities students have to do projects at undergraduate level as per the topics given in the syllabus, Teachers teach and the guide the students to carry out the projects, Many teachers are learning, enhancing and upgrading themselves by taking up research projects in various fields of environment.

Creating Awareness in the Society

Teachers and students can create awareness in the society through various ways like giving advertisements, using sign boards, showing films, through plays, involving citizens in keeping the surrounding clean, plantations, solid waste management, rainwater harvesting, caring the nature and natural resources, use of non conventional energy like solar energy, wind energy, tidal energy, biomass energy, hydrogen fuel, biodiesel, tidal energy and many more, and also regarding the sustainable development. In India National Service Scheme, Rovers and Rangers, National Cadet Corps and many number of environmental clubs are present wherein students and teachers can take part. and create awareness to public. Campaigns can be done, celebrating Vana Mahostava, World environment day,

Ecotourism and Eco Lodging

Teachers and students can take part in ecotourism for leisure and study about nature and there are many places in India where eco lodging is done, Teachers and students can stay on holidays without harming environment and learning the different habitats. The inclusion of ecotourism in ecological education and provision of ecolodge are beneficial for design of student learning outcomes, The community residents and tourist can grasp the environmental protection and education through eco lodging experiences (Kuang Sheng Liu, Sung Lin Hseuh, Han Yi Chen, 2018). Farm tourism practices and avitourism is attracting many bird watchers (Rochelle Steven, Clare Morrison, Gay Castley, July 2014)can be done.

Environmental Education and Entrepreneurs

The students have the opportunity to learn, critically think and become entrepreneurs for green products, recycling units, management of avitourism,, educational tourism based on their ideas, skills and they can also incorporate the values of environment in work or job they undertake. .

References

https://www.epa.gov/education/what-environmental-education

Kuang Sheng Liu, Sung Lin Hseuh, Han Yi Chen June (2018) Relationships between environmental education, Environmental attitudes and behavioural intentions towards eco lodging.

Rochelle Steven, Clare Morrison, Gay Castley, (2014) , Bird Watching and Avitourism -A Global Review of Research into Participant Market, Distribution and Impacts , highlighting future research priorities to inform sustainable avitourism management , Journal of sustainable tourism, 23 (8) 1257-1276

https://www.unep.org/unep-and-sdgs

Mes College of Arts Commerce and Science, Malleshwaram Bengaluru, Karnataka email : asheerabs@gmail.com

17. Plastic Waste, its Impact on Climate and Legal Framework

Dr. Rahul Tiwari

Abstract

Nowadays plastic is observed everywhere in large amounts because of its ease and also the cost. The disposal of plastic waste in the environment is a big problem due to its very low biodegradability. In many applications, plastic is virtually irreplaceable because it is cheap, strong, lightweight, and resistant to corrosion. The most common uses of plastic are in packaging and building components, such as piping. Replacing plastic with other materials is neither simple nor straightforward, mainly due to the challenge of finding an alternative that combines all the most desirable plastic properties. Biodegradable alternatives—such as special plastics, paper, or cardboard—may well have a higher greenhouse footprint because of the amount of water or natural resources consumed in their production. While plastic is durable, this also means plastic waste can be trapped in our environment for centuries, if not managed well. While plastics deteriorate into fragments easily through wear and tear, their polymer chains only break down into other smaller components at very high temperatures, such as during some chemical recycling processes. However, today only 15% of plastic waste is recycled. Awareness about the need and importance of plastic waste management among people is an alarming need of today. This paper examines the problem of the disposal of different types of plastic waste. This paper also examines the different legal frameworks available at international level for the disposal of plastic waste.

Keywords : Plastic, Microplastic, Plastic waste, Effects, Transboundary movement, Basel convention, Rotterdam Convention, Stockholm Convention,

Introduction

Plastic is a material with which humans come into contact daily. From drinking a mineral water bottle to disposing of it in the waste bin, most of the items are made up of plastic materials. Plastic word is derived from the Greek word 'Plastikos' means 'to mold'. Plastic is made up of different polymers which contain long chains of carbon. These polymers actually formed as a result of the biodegradation of organic matter which we termed fossil fuels like coal, natural gas, minerals, and plants. Plastics are strong and ductile in nature. These are poor conductors of heat and electricity which means heat and electricity cannot pass from plastic materials. Plastics are resistant to corrosion and many chemical materials.

Plastic pollution has become one of the most pressing environmental issues, as the rapidly increasing production of disposable plastic products overwhelms the world's ability to deal with them. Plastic pollution is most visible in developing Asian and African nations, where garbage collection systems are often inefficient or non-existent. But the developed world, especially in countries with low recycling rates, also has trouble properly collecting discarded plastics. Plastic trash has become so ubiquitous it has prompted efforts to write a global treaty negotiated by the United Nations.

Review of literature:

Elzafraney et al. (2005), this study has incorporated the use of recycled plastic aggregate in concrete material for a building to work out its performance with regard to thermal attributes and efficient energy performance in comparison with normal aggregate concrete. The plastic content concrete was prepared from refined highly recycled plastics to meet various requirements of building construction like strength, workability and finish ability, etc. Both buildings were subject to long- and short-term monitoring in order to determine their energy efficiencies and level of comfort. It was observed that recycled plastic concrete buildings having good insulation used 8% less energy in comparison to normal concrete; however, saving in energy was more profound in a cold climate in building with lower insulation.

L. Oyake-Ombis, B.J.M. van Vliet, and A.P.J. Mol, (2015), the authors conducted a study to assess innovations in plastic waste management in Kenya. The author found out that; there were no incentives for innovators, recycling guidelines were lacking, and working conditions were poor. With regard to plastic waste management practices, landfilling, illegal dumping and littering were prevalent in the country. The authors recommended the drafting of a plastic recycling framework by all stakeholders including those in the informal sector. This framework would include compulsory recycling targets, guidelines on the quality of plastic products, and training of informal sector workers.

M. Mourshed, M.H. Masud, F. Rashid, M.U.H. Joardder, (2017), the authors assessed the management of plastic waste in Bangladesh with the aim of recommending the best way forward. The authors noted that hindrances to effective plastic waste management in the country included poor infrastructure, lack of recycling technologies, and inadequate funds to advance waste management services. In addition, recycling and reuse were found to be minimal; with only 20% plastic waste collected while landfilling, and open and indiscriminate dumping were the predominant disposal methods. They recommended the use of alternative plastic waste management technologies such as pyrolysis, bitumen production, and the use of plastic waste as solid refuse fuel in cement kilns in addition to recycling.

Y.C. Moh, L. Abd Manaf, (2017), the authors assessed current solid waste management practices and policies in Malaysia. Their findings were that there was the limited separation of waste at source in the country hence poor recycling. In addition, the authors noted the lack of commitment by the public to participate in the initiative as well as the unavailability of accurate documented data. Open dumping and landfills were observed to be prevalent with 95% of waste being disposed of through these methods and the balance being recycled/treated or illegally dumped. In [26], the authors recommended; the regularisation of informal waste pickers, updating of waste management policies, and mandatory separation of waste at source to increase recycling rates and reduce illegal dumping incidences.

R.U. Duru, E.E. Ikpeama, and J.A. Ibekwe, (2019), the authors reviewed plastic waste management strategies in Nigeria and concluded that lack of funds and mismanagement of this limited resource and poor infrastructure hampered waste management in the country. Furthermore, over 50% of generated plastic waste is either indiscriminately dumped or in drains and waterways. The authors recommended; educating the public on the separation of waste at source; institution of fines for unsorted waste, setting up of collection centers, and WtE plants, and establishing frameworks that enhance sufficient record keeping.

Y.C. Jang, G. Lee, Y. Kwon, J. Hong Lim, J. Hyun Jeong, (2020), the authors assessed plastic packaging waste management in South Korea. Three million tonnes of plastic packaging waste were generated. The packaging waste was managed as follows; use as solid refuse fuel (39.3%), incineration without energy recovery (33.4%), recycling (13%) and the balance landfilled. The authors noted that only 22.3% of plastic packaging waste was under the EPR scheme and therefore they advocated for the list of plastic items covered by EPR to be expanded to reduce plastic pollution.

C. Liu, T. Thang Nguyen, Y. Ishimura, (2021), the authors investigated SUP waste management in Hanoi, Vietnam, and described the secondary use of plastic shopping bags as bin liners after a single use. In addition, although plastic bags should be taxed, implementation is lacking. Landfilling was found to be prevalent while recycling is limited. According to the authors, there are gaps in drafted waste management policies that need to be addressed.

Objectives of the Study :

These are the objectives of the research paper: -

1. To study the scope of the global plastic waste challenge;
2. To study the linkages between plastic waste and climate change;
3. To study the causes and impacts of unsound management of plastic waste;
4. To study the legal frameworks available at the international level for the disposal of plastic waste.

Statement of the Problem :

Most plastic products are only used once (e.g. cups, plates, takeaway containers, and bags). Others can be used for several years (e.g. certain storage containers). In other applications, plastics may have relatively long life spans, ranging from approximately 5 years (e.g.

textiles and electronic equipment) to more than 20 years (e.g. industrial machinery and construction materials). Of the plastic waste generated globally to date, only about 9% has been recycled and only about 12% has been incinerated. The remaining 79% has been disposed in landfills or released into the environment. The commonly used plastics are not biodegradable. As a result, if not managed in an environmentally sound manner they accumulate in uncontrolled landfills or the environment. Moreover, they slowly decompose to form microplastics.

Significance of the study :

This paper will help to enhance the knowledge about the problem of plastic waste management and also spread awareness regarding the problems that occurred due to the use of plastic materials. This paper will also provide knowledge regarding the international conventions of plastic waste management. This paper will benefit and help the future researchers with their guidance.

Methodology :

A method is a way of approaching the problem. The truth involved in a problem can be found only by following systematic steps. The type of steps to be applied depends on the object and the nature of the problem. Research methodology is a process that is used to collect new information or data regarding the problem of research. This process of research methodology is systematic. Methodology, in reality, covers the blueprint of research and played a significant role in any research. Research methodology provides such values or ethics that are necessary for the research outcome. Any research required a deep study of the research problem. This paper has used doctrinal or non-empirical research methodology to achieve the objectives of this paper. Doctrinal or non-empirical research methodology is a research methodology that has been based on legal propositions. This research methodology has been used to analyse the present legal provisions or case laws by using legal reasoning power to find out the solution to the research problem. It includes an analysis of existing statutory provisions, reports, articles, books, journals, and cases.

Introduction of Plastic :

The first fully synthetic plastic was invented in 1907. Since the 1950s, the use of plastic has grown rapidly. Plastic refers to a wide range of artificial substances which use polymers as a main ingredient and can be shaped when soft into many different forms. Plastic can be made from a range of organic polymers. However, 97-99% of plastic is made from hydrocarbons, mostly oil and natural gases which cannot be renewable. Versatility, strength, lightness, and low cost made plastic a revolutionary material with potential uses in a wide variety of appliances. Plastic can be used for a wide variety of appliances. Examples are shopping bags, food packaging, cars, spacecraft, electronic equipment, and water purifiers. The packaging sector accounts for almost half of global plastic consumption. Plastic consumption is also significant in:

- Building and construction (e.g. pipes, paints, flooring, sealants)
- Transport (e.g. wear and tear on tyres, road surfaces, and markings)
- Electric and electronic products (e.g. smartphones, televisions)
- Industrial machinery
- Agriculture (e.g. irrigation pipelines, greenhouse covering materials, pellets for the delivery of chemicals)
- Health and personal care

Types of Plastics and their Utilities :

The numerous types of plastics and their utilities are as follows:

Thermoplastics :

Thermoplastics are a type of polymer that can be melted and reshaped multiple times by the application of heat and pressure. They are widely used in many different industries because of their versatility, durability, and ease of processing. Some common examples of thermoplastics with their utilities and characteristics are as follows: -

Polyethylene Terephthalate (PET) :

Polyethylene terephthalate (PET) is a polymer of thermoplastic that is commonly used in the manufacture of a variety of products, including wrapping materials, fabrics, films, and bottles. It is a type of polyester and is made by combining terephthalic acid and ethylene glycol. Although PET is a versatile and useful material, its production and disposal can have negative environmental impacts.

High-density Polyethylene (HDPE) :

High-density polyethylene (HDPE) is a polymer plastic that is a petroleum product. It is generally used in a wide diversity of applications because of its strength, durability, and resistance to chemicals, moisture, and impact.

HDPE is produced by the polymerization of ethylene, which is a colourless and odourless gas. The polymerization process creates long chains of ethylene molecules that are linked together to form a solid material with a high density.

Polyvinyl Chloride (PVC) :

Polyvinyl chloride (PVC) is a synthetic plastic polymer made from the monomer vinyl chloride. PVC is widely used in construction materials, packaging, medical devices, and a variety of other applications.

PVC is a thermoplastic material, which means that it can be melted and reformed repeatedly without significant degradation. It is also known for its high durability, resistance to chemicals, and ability to maintain its shape under stress. However, PVC is not biodegradable and can release toxic fumes if burned.

In its rigid form, PVC is commonly used in pipes, fittings, and window frames. Flexible PVC is often used in inflatable products, such as pool toys and air mattresses, as well as in medical tubing and IV bags. PVC can also be found in various domestic products using daily life, including shower curtains, flooring, and electrical wire insulation.

Low-density Polyethylene (LDPE) :

Low-density polyethylene (LDPE) is a form of thermoplastic and it is a product of monomer ethylene. It is a polymer with a high degree of branching and a relatively low density, which makes it more flexible and less dense than other types of polyethylene.

LDPE is commonly used in various products of daily needs, including packaging films, plastic bags, squeeze bottles, wire and cable insulation, toys, and many other consumer and industrial products. It is known for its high clarity, good chemical resistance, and good impact strength, making it a popular choice for packaging and other applications where flexibility and durability are important.

LDPE is also known for its recyclability, and it can be recycled into a variety of products, including new plastic products, plastic lumber, and more. It is often identified by the recycling symbol with the number 4 inside, which is typically found on the bottom of plastic containers.

Polypropylene (PP) :

Polypropylene (PP) is a form of thermoplastic polymer that is commonly used in various products for daily needs due to its versatility, durability, and chemical resistance. It is a member of the polyolefin family of polymers, which also includes polyethylene.

Some common applications of polypropylene include packaging materials (such as bottles, containers, and bags), automotive parts, textiles (such as carpets and clothing), and medical devices. It is also used in a variety of other industries, including construction, electronics, and agriculture.

Polystyrene (PS) :

Polystyrene is a form of synthetic polymer and it is made from the monomer styrene. It is a thermoplastic material that can be molded into various shapes when heated. Polystyrene is widely used in many industries, including packaging, automotive, electronics, and, construction due to its excellent insulating properties, light weight, and low cost.

Polystyrene can be produced in two forms: solid and foam. Solid polystyrene is used in products such as disposable cutlery, CD cases, and laboratory equipment. Foam polystyrene, also known as expanded polystyrene (EPS), is used in packaging materials, insulation, and foam cups and plates.

Polystyrene can survive in the environment for a very long time, although it is not easily biodegradable. It can also be a source of pollution when not properly disposed of. As a result, there is growing concern about its environmental impact, and efforts are being made to find more sustainable alternatives.

Polyurethane (PU) :

Polyurethane is a polymer made from the reaction between a polyol (a type of alcohol with multiple hydroxyl groups) and an isocyanate. The resulting polymer can be a thermoplastic or thermosetting material, depending on the specific formulation and manufacturing process.

Polyurethane is a versatile material with a wide range of applications, including foams, coatings, adhesives, elastomers, and fibers. It is used in a variety of industries, including construction, automotive, furniture, and textiles.

Others Plastics :

There are numerous other types of plastics except these six types, often used in the engineering sector. Examples include nylon, acrylonitrile butadiene styrene (ABS), and polycarbonate (PC).

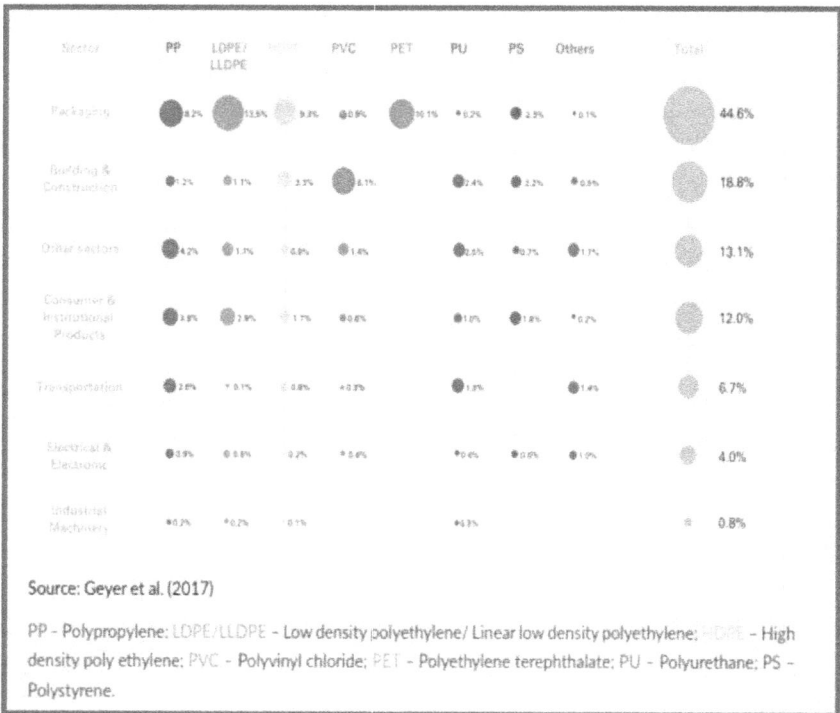

Sector	PP	LDPE/ LLDPE		PVC	PET	PU	PS	Others	Total
Packaging	8.2%	13.5%	9.3%	0.9%	10.1%	0.2%	2.3%	0.1%	44.6%
Building & Construction	1.2%	1.1%	3.3%	8.1%		2.4%	2.2%	0.5%	18.8%
Other sectors	4.2%	1.1%	0.9%	1.4%		2.6%	0.7%	1.1%	13.1%
Consumer & Institutional Products	3.8%	2.9%	1.1%	0.6%		1.8%	1.8%	0.2%	12.0%
Transportation	2.6%	0.1%	0.8%	0.3%		1.3%		1.4%	6.7%
Electrical & Electronic	0.9%	0.8%	0.2%	0.6%		0.6%	0.6%	1.0%	4.0%
Industrial Machinery	0.2%	0.2%	0.1%			0.3%			0.8%

Source: Geyer et al. (2017)

PP - Polypropylene; LDPE/LLDPE - Low density polyethylene/ Linear low density polyethylene; HDPE - High density poly ethylene; PVC - Polyvinyl chloride; PET - Polyethylene terephthalate; PU - Polyurethane; PS - Polystyrene.

Estimate global polymer consumption by type and sector

Microplastics :

Microplastics are small plastic particles that measure less than 5 millimeters in size. They can be formed either intentionally during the manufacturing process of certain products or can be the result of the breakdown of larger plastic items due to weathering, mechanical action, or ultraviolet radiation. The numerous types of microplastics and their major utilities are as follows:

Primary Microplastics :

Small plastic particles are known as Primary microplastics that are intentionally produced for use in various consumer and industrial products, as opposed to secondary microplastics are the product that is formed from the collapse of larger plastic products.

Secondary Microplastics:

Secondary microplastics are product that is formed from the collapse of larger plastic products or items. Unlike primary microplastics, which are purposefully mass-produced at a small size, secondary microplastics are a product of environmental degradation, such as the weathering, fragmentation, and degradation of plastic waste.

Microbeads :

Tiny plastic particles are known as Microbeads, typically smaller than 5mm in diameter that is used in various cosmetic product of personal care, such as exfoliating scrubs, toothpaste, and body washes. These microbeads are made of polyethylene, polypropylene, or other polymers, and are designed to be washed down the drain after use. (e.g. scrubs and toothpastes).

Effects of Plastic Waste :

There are a lot of adverse effects of plastic waste. Some major adverse effects of plastic waste are as follows:

Effects on the Environment :

As plastic waste often contains hazardous substances, it can not only have adverse physical but also chemical effects on animals. Both marine and terrestrial animals may be entangled in plastic waste or ingest plastic waste. Ingestion can block their digestive tracts and may cause exposure to hazardous additives contained in plastic waste.

Microplastics can come from a various source, including the collapse of larger plastic items, microbeads in personal care products, and synthetic fibers from clothing. Concern is developing over the harmful consequences of microplastics on both human health and the environment. Overall, the effects of microplastics are a complex and evolving area of study. However, it is clear that microplastics can have negative impacts on human health, the economy, and the environment, and efforts are underway to better understand and mitigate these impacts.

Plastic waste also harms ecosystems. It can serve as a host for transporting invasive species long distances. Moreover, plastic waste can adversely affect habitats such as coral reefs, mudflats, and mangroves.

Effects on Human Health :

Micro- and nano-plastics have already made their way through the food chain and on our plates. They can be found in seafood, water, and salt, to name a few. Moreover, plastic can be found in the air we breathe and even enters our bodies via absorption through the skin. It subsequently accumulates in our organs, including the placenta. There is substantial evidence that plastics associated chemicals such as plasticizers and flame retardants enter the human body and are associated with serious health impacts, especially in women. There is also evidence that floating plastics transport pharmaceutical, other bioactive chemical and endocrine disrupting waste as well as pathogenic bacteria to coastal areas, with known impacts on ecosystems and human health.

Air Pollution :

The uncontrolled burning of plastic waste is known to generate harmful emissions which can have a direct health impact on people and animals.

Climate Change :

There are two types of climate change impacts associated with plastic waste:

1. Emissions generated during plastics production, can be partially offset via recycling.

2. Emissions associated with the management of plastic waste materials.

The production and dumping of plastic waste materials also have a significant impact on climate change. Non-renewable resources, such as significant quantities of fossil fuels, oil, and natural gas, which are linked to greenhouse gas emissions, are needed for the production of plastic. The transportation of plastic products and waste also adds to these emissions.

Furthermore, plastic waste management can also contribute to climate change. For instance, burning plastic trash in open-air incinerators or landfills may result in the release of greenhouse gases like carbon dioxide (CO_2) and methane (CH_4).

Global emissions from the incineration of plastic packaging waste totalled 16 million metric tons of CO_2 in 2015. Recent research suggests that the climate change effects associated with uncontrolled open burning of plastic waste lead to a yet far higher climate change impact.

Economic and Social Impacts :

Plastic pollution is also detrimental to the amenity value of the natural environment. This has a direct cost – e.g., in the form of the cost of cleaning activities – but also has wider socio-economic effects. For example, plastic pollution has been shown to have significant negative effects on tourism. Plastic waste can also block drainage systems, creating unsanitary conditions allowing the vectors of disease to flourish and leading to flooding.

Legal Framework on Hazardous Wastes:

Hazardous waste is regulated by a variety of legal frameworks around the world, including international agreements, regional treaties, and national legislation. The following are some of the major legal frameworks related to hazardous waste:

Basel Convention :

The Basel Convention, also known as the Convention for the Control of Transboundary Movements of Hazardous Wastes and the Disposal of Such Hazardous Wastes, is an international treaty with the goals of reducing the movement of hazardous waste between two or more countries and ensuring that such waste is disposed of safely and environmentally soundly. The Agreement outlines a variety of responsibilities for parties to control the production, transportation, and disposal of hazardous waste as well as to make sure that such trash is not delivered to developing nations without their permission. The provisions of the Basel Convention can be structured around three main pillars:

1. Regulation of transboundary activities of harmful and other wastes.
2. Advancement of environmentally complete management of harmful and other wastes.
3. Preclusion and minimization of the production of harmful and other wastes.

The Conference of the nations to the Basel Convention adopted two important decisions to advance prevention and minimization:

Cartagena Declaration :

The 16th Ordinary Conference of the Contracting States to the Convention for the Preservation of the Marine Environment and the Coastal Area of the Mediterranean, generally known as the Barcelona Convention, adopted the Cartagena Declaration on Marine Litter in the Mediterranean in December 2011.

The Declaration was developed to address the growing problem of marine litter in the Mediterranean region, particularly plastic waste. It acknowledges the significant threat that marine litter poses to the environment, human health, and economic activities such as tourism and fisheries.

Overall, the Cartagena Declaration is an important step towards addressing the increasing problem of plastic waste and marine litter in the Mediterranean region and represents a commitment by stakeholders to take action to guard the marine environment and coastal communities.

Waste Amendments to the Basel Convention :

The Basel Convention is a global accord that aims to reduce the flow of hazardous waste between two or more countries, particularly between wealthy and poor nations. The convention was first adopted in 1989 and has been amended several times since then. The Ban Amendment, which was adopted in 1995 and becomes effective in 2019, is the most recent change to the Basel Convention.

The Ban Amendment prohibits the export of hazardous waste from being settled to emerging countries for any reason, including recycling or disposal. This amendment was proposed in response to concerns that developed countries were exporting their harmful waste to emerging countries, where environmental and human health protections may be weaker.

Other Amendments to the Basel Convention Include :

- Guidelines for liability and compensation for the harm resulting from such transboundary movements of hazardous waste are established by the Basel Protocol on Responsibility and Compensation for Damage Resulting from Transboundary Movements of Hazardous Wastes and their Disposal, which was adopted in 1999.

- The Basel Convention Amendment, which was passed in 2015, enhances the regulations governing the transboundary movement of hazardous waste, notably electronic trash.

- The Plastic Waste Amendment, adopted in 2019, aims to reduce the environmental impact of plastic waste by controlling its transboundary movement and promoting its environmentally sound management.

Overall, the Basel Convention and its amendments seek to minimize the risks associated with the transboundary movement of harmful waste and promote the environmentally sound management of waste.

The Rotterdam Convention :

An international agreement known as the Rotterdam Convention attempts to preserve the environment and human health by promoting responsible trade in dangerous chemicals and pesticides.

The convention was amended in 2021 to expand its purview to include plastic trash. The amendment seeks to control transnational migrations of plastic trash, notably from industrialised to developing nations, and to advance the environmentally responsible treatment of plastic garbage.

Under the amendment, exporters of plastic waste will be required to obtain the prior informed consent of the importing country before shipping the waste. The importing country will have the right to refuse the waste if it is deemed to pose a risk to human health or the environment, or if it cannot be managed in an environmentally sound way.

The Rotterdam Convention on plastic waste is a significant step toward addressing the global plastic waste crisis and reducing the effect of plastic waste on the atmosphere and human health. However, it will require the cooperation of all countries to be effective, and it remains to be seen how well it will be implemented in practice.

The Stockholm Convention :

A category of extremely dangerous compounds known as POPs are the focus of the Stockholm Convention on Persistent Organic Pollutants (POPs), an international agreement that attempts to eliminate or regulate their production, use, and emission. POPs are hazardous pollutants that pose a major threat to both the environment and human health because they are persistent in the environment and bioaccumulate in the food chain. According to the Stockholm Agreement, countries must take steps to prevent or drastically restrict the emission of POPs into the environment. Plastic additives regulated by the Stockholm Convention include brominated flame retardants, such as hexabromobiphenyl, commercial penta-, octa- and decabromodiphenyl ether, hexabromocyclododecane; fluorinated substances, such as perfluorooctanoic acid (PFOA) and perfluoro octane sulfonic acid (PFOS); and chlorinated substances, such as short chain chlorinated paraffin and polychlorinated naphthalenes.

European Union :

The European Union has developed a range of directives and regulations to regulate hazardous waste management across its member states. The Waste Framework Directive, which lays out a broad framework for the management of waste, including hazardous waste, is the most significant piece of legislation. The EU also has specific regulations to govern the classification, labeling, packaging, transport, and disposal of hazardous waste.

United States :

The Resource Conservation and Recovery Act (RCRA), which lays out a thorough framework for the management of hazardous waste from cradle to grave, regulates hazardous waste in the United States. The RCRA requires facilities that generate, transport, or dispose of hazardous waste to obtain permits, and sets out specific requirements for the handling, storage, and disposal of such waste.

Conclusion :

The need to address the problem of plastic waste is becoming more widely recognised. Moreover, a fix is required for the deficient waste management systems. Currently, efficient trash collection and disposal are inaccessible to more than 30% of the world's population.

There is no silver bullet or magic stick to make a solution for this problem. There are many other legal frameworks at national and international levels that regulate hazardous waste management. These frameworks frequently work to reduce waste generation, promote waste reduction, and encourage the recycling and reuse of waste materials in order to safeguard human health and the environment from the adverse effects of hazardous waste and to promote sustainable development.

Concurrently, we need to scale and build other solutions. All of these initiatives work to keep plastic garbage out of the environment and advance the circular economy, which unlocks the value of waste. Although it's a challenging endeavour, it can definitely be accomplished with cooperation.

References:
i. L. Oyake-Ombis, B.J.M. van Vliet, A.P.J. Mol, "Managing plastic waste in East Africa: Niche innovations in plastic

production and solid waste," Habitat International, 48, 188–197, 2015.

ii. M. Mourshed, M.H. Masud, F. Rashid, M.U.H. Joardder, Towards the effective plastic waste management in Bangladesh: a review, Environmental Science and Pollution Research, 24(35), 27021–27046, 2017.

iii. Y.C. Moh, L. Abd Manaf, "Solid waste management transformation and future challenges of source separation and recycling practice in Malaysia," Resources, Conservation and Recycling, 116(2017), 1–14, 2017.

iv. R.U. Duru, E.E. Ikpeama, J.A. Ibekwe, "Challenges and prospects of plastic waste management in Nigeria," Waste Disposal & Sustainable Energy, 1(2), 117–126, 2019.

v. Y.C. Jang, G. Lee, Y. Kwon, J. Hong Lim, J. Hyun Jeong, "Recycling and management practices of plastic packaging waste towards a circular economy in South Korea," Resources, Conservation and Recycling, 158, 104798, 2020.

vi. C. Liu, T. Thang Nguyen, Y. Ishimura, "Current situation and key challenges on the use of single-use plastic in Hanoi," Waste Management, 121, 422–431, 2021.

vii. htpp/WASTE%20&%20BASEL%20CONV/BC_Introductory%20lesson.pdf.

viii. htpp/WASTE%20&%20BASEL%20CONV/BC_Lesson%201.pdf

ix. htpp/WASTE%20&%20BASEL%20CONV/BC_Lesson%202.pdf

x. htpp/WASTE%20&%20BASEL%20CONV/BC_Lesson%203.pdf

Assistant Professor,
Atal Bihari Vajpayee School of Legal Studies,
C.S.J.M. University (Formerly Kanpur University),
Kanpur, Uttar Pradesh.

18. Phytochemical Characterization of *Triticum Aestivum* (Wheat Grass)

Punithavtahi Manogaran, Devi Vijayavarma

Abstract

Many drugs commonly used today are of herbal origin. Some are made from plant extracts; others are synthesized to mimic a natural plant compound. Wheatgrass (*Triticum aestivum* L.) is one of the most widely used health foods, but its functional groups and mechanisms remain unidentified. Wheat germinated over a period of 6-10 days is generally called wheatgrass. During germination, vitamins, minerals, and phenolic compounds including flavonoids are synthesized in wheat sprouts. The present study was designed to evaluate relative contribution of different phytochemicals in various extracts of wheat grass; the leaves of the selected medicinal plant were washed, air dried and then powdered. The various extract of leaves sample was used for the phytochemical analysis to find out the phytochemical constituents in the plant. Phytochemical analysis results of this medicinal plant showed the presence of terpenoids, flavonoids and alkaloids were found. Qualitative phytochemical analysis of this plant confirms the presence of various phytochemicals like alkaloids, flavonoids, tannins, terpenoids, steroids, and glycosides in their methanolic leaves extract. The present study dealt with highlighting of the phytochemicals with respect to the role of this plant in traditional medicinal system. The phytochemical analysis of the plants is very important commercially and has great interest in pharmaceutical companies for the production of the new drugs for curing of various diseases. It is expected that the important phytochemical properties recognized by our study in this indigenous medicinal plant will be very useful in the pharmacological field.

Keywords : Wheatgrass, phytochemical, qualitative, analysis

Introduction

Plant Medicine, sometimes referred to as Herbalism or Botanical Medicine, is the use of herbs for their therapeutic or medicinal value. An herb is a plant or plant part valued for its medicinal, aromatic or savory qualities. Herb plants produce and contain a variety of active substances that act upon the body. Preliminary screening of phytochemicals is a valuable step in the detection of bioactive principles present in medicinal plants and may lead to novel environmental friendly bioherbicides and drug discovery.

Wheat, (Triticum species) a cereal grass of the Gramineae (Poaceae) family, is the world's most edible grain cereal-grass crop. Nowadays, researchers have known Wheat grass is a nutrient-rich type of young grass in the wheat family , is many times richer in levels of vitamins, minerals and proteins as compared to seed kernel, or grain products of the mature cereal plant (Tirgar1 PR) . At present, wheatgrass is quickly becoming one of the most widely used supplemental health foods and is available in many health food stores as fresh produce, tablets, frozen juice, and powder. Wheatgrass provides a concentrated amount of nutrients, including iron; calcium; magnesium; amino acids; and vitamins A, C and E and large amounts (70%) of chlorophyll (Hui Ming Yu et al). Some proponents tout wheatgrass as a treatment for cancer (Keong Ys), ulcerative colitis (Ben Arye E) and joint pain, and also serve as antioxidant (Das A). It has been suggested that wheatgrass has a greater nutritional value than several everyday foods, and ingesting wheatgrass is comparable to eating a large amount of vegetables (T Harvey). In their study, Marwaha et al had thalassemia patients drink wheatgrass juice daily, and as a result, half required over 25% less packed red blood cells.

The effectiveness of the plant extracts is mainly due to the presence of bioactive constituents like phenolics, flavonoids and others (Kim DK). During germination, vitamins, minerals, and phenolic compounds including flavonoids are synthesized in wheat sprouts, and wheat sprouts reach the maximum antioxidant potential (Acharya R). Wheatgrass is used to treat many conditions, but so far there isn't enough scientific evidence to support effectiveness for any of these uses. By this study, we have embodied the most effective solvent extract of wheat grass, to determine the total phenolic and flavonoid and other phytochemical contents. Details on the qualitative and quantitative compositions of various solvent extracts of wheatgrass would provide useful information on therapeutic use.

Materials and Methods

Cultivation of *Triticum Aestivum*

Wheat, (*Triticum* species) a cereal grass of the Gramineae (*Poaceae)* family, is the world's largest edible grain cereal- grass crop. The wheat plant is an annual grass. In early growth stages the wheat plant consists of a much-compressed stem or crown and numerous narrowly linear or linear-lanceolate leaves.

Extraction of Plant Material

The nineth day grass of *Triticum aestivum* was cultivated, collected and chopped with the help of knife. It was dried in shade and then powdered with a mechanical grinder. The powder was passed through sieve and stored in a labeled air tight container for further studies. Wheatgrass powder was subjected to soxhlet extraction by using various solvents like double distilled water, methanol, ethylacetate and chloroform for about 24h. Each solvent extract was evaporated to dryness.

Qualitative Screening

Carbohydrates : In a test tube containing 2.0 ml of plant sample, 2 drops of freshly prepared 20% alcoholic solution of a naphthol was added and mixed. To this solution 2.0 ml of concentrated sulphuric acid was added so as to form a layer below the mixture, formation of the red violet ring at the junction of the solution and its disappearance on the addition of an excess of alkali solution indicate the presence of carbohydrates.

Proteins : 1 part of mercury was digested with 2 parts of HNO3 and the resulting solution was diluted with 2 volumes of water. To a small quantity of decoction, 5-6 drops of Million's reagent was added. A precipitate which turned red on heating was formed and it indicates the presence of proteins.

Alkaloids : 1.36gm of mercuric chloride was dissolved in 60ml distilled water and 5gm of potassium iodide and diluted to 100ml with distilled water. To 1.0ml of acidic aqueous solution of samples, few drops of reagent were added. Formation of white or pale precipitate showed the presence of alkaloids (Harborne, 1973).

Flavonoids : In a test tube containing 0.5ml of various extracts of the samples, 5-10 drops of dilute HCl and a small piece of Zn or

Mg were added and then solution was boiled for few minutes. In the presence of flavonoids, the reddish pink or dirty brown colour was produced (Harborne, 1973).

Tannins : In a test tube containing about 5.0 ml of an various extract, a few drops of 1% solution of lead acetate was added. A yellow or red colour precipitate was formed, indicating the presence of tannins (Harborne, 1973).

Phenols : To 1.0ml of alcoholic solution of samples, 2.0 ml of distilled water followed by a few drops of 10% aqueous ferric chloride solution were added and the formation of blue or green colour indicates the presence of phenols (Harborne, 1973).

Saponins : In a test tube containing 5ml of various extract of sample, a few drops of sodium bicarbonate was added. The mixture was shaken vigorously for 3mins. A honey comb like froth was formed and it showed the presence of saponins (Harborne, 1973).

Glycosides : A small amount of various extract of sample was dissolved in 1ml of water and aqueous solution of sodium hydroxide was added. Formation of a yellow colour indicates the presence of glycosides (Harborne, 1973).

Steroids : To 2.0ml of various extracts of samples, 1.0 ml of concentrated H_2SO_4 was added carefully along the sides of the test tube. Formation of red colour chloroform layer indicates the presence of steroids (Harborne, 1973).

Terpenoids : 0.5 ml of extract was mixed with 2 ml of chloroform in a test tube. 3 ml of concentrated sulfuric acid was carefully added to the mixture to form a layer. A reddish brown coloration was formed for the presence of terpenoids.

Quantitative Analysis

Chemicals : Vanillin reagent -1% vanillin in 70% conc.H_2SO_4, Catechin standard 110 µg/ml, Ethanol (80%), Folin-Ciocalteau reagent (1N), Sodium carbonate (20%), Standard gallic acid solution (100µg/ml in water).

Estimation of Total Carbohydrate : The total carbohydrate content was estimated by the method of Hedge and Hofreiter, 1962.

Estimation of Protein : The total Protein content was estimated by the Lowry's method.

Estimation of Alkaloids : Total alkaloids was measured by the method of Harborne, 1973

Estimation of Phenols : The amount of total phenols was estimated by the method proposed by Mallick and Singh (1980).

Results & Discussion

Plant are endowed with various phytochemical molecules such as vitamins, terpenoids, phenolics, lignins, tannins, flavonoids, quinines, alkaloids, and other metabolites, which are rich in antioxidant activity (Wei Zheng, Shiow Y Wang) . Studies have shown that many of the phytocompounds possess anti-inflammatory, anti-diabetic and antimicrobial activities (joan)   . In recent years, secondary plant metabolites (phytochemicals), previously with unknown pharmacological activities, have been extensively investigated as a source of medicinal agents (Alluri V Krishnaraju) .

Plant derived substances have recently become a great interest owing to the versatile applications. Medicinal plants and herbs are the richest bio-resource of drugs of traditional systems of medicine, modern medicine, pharmaceutical intermediates and chemical entities for synthetic drugs.

Table 1: Phytochemical screening of *Triticum aestivum*

S.No	Parameters	Methanol	Ethylacetate	Chloroform	Aqueous
1	Carbohydrates	+	+	+	+
2	Proteins	+	-	-	+
3	Alkaloids	+	-	-	+
4	Flavonoids	+	-	-	-
5	Tannins	+	-	-	+
6	Phenols	+	-	-	+
7	Saponins	-	-	+	+
8	Glycosides	+	-	-	+
9	Steroids	+	-	-	-
10	Terpenoids	+	-	-	-

(+)=indicates presence of compounds (-)=indicates absence of compounds Phytochemical screening of *Triticum aestivum* using various extracts like aqueous, methanol, ethylacetate and chloroform. Phytochemical qualitative analysis of *Triticum aestivum* presented in the Table 1.

The screening analysis was performed in order to identify various secondary metabolites which is present in *Triticum aestivum* using a wide range of solvents namely aqueous, methanol, ethyl acetate and chloroform.

The screening analysis of *Triticum aestivum* using various solvents revealed the presence of carbohydrate, protein alkaloids, tannins, phenols, in the methanolic and aqueous extracts. While the presence of saponins was noted in chloroform extract. The result of our present study is further supported with similar studies reported by Gaurav Kumar *et al*.

The qualitative phytochemical analysis results explored the presence of a wide range of phytochemical constituents which signifies the *Triticum aestivum* as a valuable therapeutic natural source which will serve as an effective herbal option to compact dreadful infectious diseases.

Table 2: Quantitative analysis of *Triticum Aestivum*

Species	Carbohydrates (mg/g)	Proteins (mg/g)	Alkaloids (mg/g)	Phenols (mg/g)
Triticum	164.0	120.0	150.0	0.50

The level of carbohydrate in *Triticum aestivum* (extract) is represented in the above table. It was found to be 164.0 mg/g. Carbohydrate is a biological molecule consisting of carbon, hydrogen, and oxygen atoms on the basis of mass, the carbohydrates are the most abundant class of biomolecule in nature. They occur as food reserves in the liver and muscles of animals. In addition, they are the important source of energy required for the various metabolic activities of the living organisms. Plants are richer source of carbohydrates in comparison to the animals. The polysaccharides serves as storage of energy (starch and glycogen) and also as structural components (cellulose and chitin). The derivatives of carbohydrate performs main other important key roles in the immune system, fertilization process, preventing pathogenesis, blood dotting and development.

The presence of good store of carbohydrates in *Triticum aestivum* reveals the efficacy of *Triticum aestivum* as the phytochemicals store. The results of our work goes in accordance with report of Shirude Anup Asokh. The level of protein in *Triticum aestivum* (extract) is represented in the above table. It was found to be 120.0 mg/g. Proteins occur in every part of the cell and constitute about 50% of the cellular dry weight. It perform a wide variety of specialized and essential functions in the living cells (Satyanarayana.U and Chakrapani.U., 2011). The results of our present study is further supported with the similar reports presented by Shirude Anup Asokh. The level of alkaloids in *Triticum aestivum* (extract) is represented in the above table. It was found to be 150 mg/g. Many alkaloids are poisonous some are used clinically and others are additives. They are used as analgesics, antimalarial, antihypertensive, cough depressant, hyper glycemic agents etc

The results of our present study is further supported with the similar reports presented by the University of Plymouth. The level of phenols in *Triticum aestivum* (extract) is represented in the above table. It was found to be 0.50 mg/g. Phenolic compounds are secondary products which possess an aromatic ring bearing a hidroxyl substituent and most are of plant origin. Phenolic compounds are physiologically active against herbivores or pathogens are now used as pharmaceuticals, herbicides etc (Elmas Özeker., 1999) and are reported to have antioxidant activity(Marja P Ka) The results of the present work is further substantiated with the report of Gaurav Kumar.

Conclusion

Scientific research is increasingly confirming what was known to our ancestors form experience. While plants continued to provide us pleasure with their beauty (colour and fragrance) and enhance the taste of our food by their flavour, we seemed to have become moreish. Young cereal plants were valued in ancient times. It had been said that people in the ancient Middle East ate the green leaf tips of the wheat plant as a delicacy (Gaurav Kumar). It helps to prevent tooth disorders, constipation, skin diseases etc (Manisha Vats).

With this wide potential, medicinal application and therapeutic value, the present work has been undertaken and the inferences are summarized as follows.

- Phytochemical qualitative screening exhibited a good range of primary metabolites and a wide range of secondary metabolites (alkaloids, tannins, phenols, saponins and glycosides) present in *Triticum aestivum*..
- The quantification of Alkaloids (150mg/g) and Phenols (0.5mg/g) indicates the quantum store of valuable secondary metabolites compounds in *Triticum aestivum*.

Herbs are staging comeback and 'herbal renaissance' is happening all over the globe, the herbal products today. symbolize safety in contrast to the synthetic drugs that are regarded as unsafe to human and environment. Although, herbs had been raised for the medicinal, flavoring and aromatic qualities for centuries. The synthetic products of the modern age surpassed their importance for a while. However, the blind dependence on synthetic drug is over and people are retaining to the natural with hope of safety and security. With this rational evidence and on scientific basis, hence study justify and supports the use of *Triticum aestivum* in traditional folk medicine.

References

1. Tirgar1 PR, Thumber BL, Desai TR. (2011) Isolation, Characterization and Biological Evaluation of Iron Chelator from Triticum Aestivum (Wheat Grass). International Journal of Pharma and Bio Sciences.; 2:288-296

2. Chia-Che Tsai, Chih-Ru Lin, Hsien-Yu Tsai, Chia-Jung Chen, Wen-Tai Li, Hui-Ming Yu *et al.(2013).*The journal of biological chemistry; 288:17689-17697.

3. Alitheen NB, Oon CL, Keong YS, Chuan TK, Li HK, Yong HW.(2011); Cytotoxic effects of commercial wheatgrass and fiber towards human acute promyelocytic leukemia cells (HL60). Pak. J Pharm Sci. 24:243-250.

4. Das A, Raychaudhuri U, Chakraborty R. (2012) Effect of freeze drying and oven drying on antioxidant properties of fresh wheatgrass. Int. J. Food Sci. Nutr.,; 63:718-721.

5. Ben-Arye E, Goldin E, Wengrower D, Stamper A, Kohn R, Berry E. (2002) Wheat grass juice in the treatment of active distal ulcerative colitis. Arandomized double-blind placebo-controlled trial. Scand. J Gastroenterol. 37:444-449.

6. Chon SU, Heo BG, Park YS, Kim DK, Gorinstein S.(2009); Total phenolics level, antioxidant activities and cytotoxicity of young sprouts of some traditional Korean salad plants. Plant Foods for Hum Nutr. 64:25-31.

7. Garima Shakya, Sankar Pajaniradje, Muddasarul Hoda, Varalakshmi Durairaj, Rukkumani Rajagopalan. GC-MS Analysis, *In Vitro* Antioxidant and Cytotoxic Studies of Wheatgrass Extract. American Journal of Phytomedicine and Clinical Therapeutics. 7:877-893.

8. Kulkarni SD, Tilak JC, Acharya R, Rajurkar NS, Devasagayam TPA, Reddy AVR, (2006). Evaluation of the antioxidant activity of wheatgrass (Triticum aestivum L.) as a function of growth under different conditions. Phytother Res. 20:218-27.

9. M Handzel, J Sibert, T Harvey, H Deshmukh (2008); C Chambers. Monitoring the Oxygenation of Blood during Exercise after Ingesting Wheatgrass Juice. The Internet Journal of Alternative Medicine. 8:1.

10. Marwaha RK, Deepak B, Siftinder K, Amita T. (2004) Wheat Grass Juice Reduces Transfusion Requirement in Patients with Thalassemia Major: A Pilot Study. Indian Pediatr; 41:716-720.

11. Wei Zheng, Shiow Y Wang (2001). Antioxidant Activity and Phenolic Compounds in Selected Herbs. Journal of Agricultural and Food Chemistry; 49:5165-5170.
12. Joan IA, Campbell-Tofte , Per Molgaard, Kaj Winther (2012) Harnessing the Potential Clinical Use of Medicinal Plants as Anti-Diabetic Agents. Botanics: Targets and Therapy2:7-19.
13. Alluri V Krishnaraju, Tayi VN Rao, Dodda Sundararaju, Mulabagal Vanisree, Hsin-Sheng Tsay, Gottumukkala V Subbaraju (2005) Assessment of Bioactivity of Indian Medicinal Plants Using Brine Shrimp (Artemia salina) Lethality Assay. International Journal of Applied Science and Engineering; 3:125-134.
14. Gaurav Kumar, Loganathan Karthik, Kokati Venkata Bhaskara Rao (2010) Antibacterial Activity of Aqueous Extract of Calotropis Gigantea Leaves–An In Vitro Study. International Journal of Pharmaceutical Sciences Review and Research; 4:141-144.
15. Shirude Anup Asokh. Phytochemical and Pharmacological Screening of Wheat Grass Juice *(Triticum Aestivum L.).(*2011) International Journal of Pharmaceutical Sciences Review and Research.; 9:159-164.
16. Satyanarayana U, Chakrapani U. (2011) Biochemistry (43). Kolkata. Third Reprinted Edition. Books and Allied (P) Ltd
17. Jack G Woolley. Plant Alkaloids. (2 0 1 1) Encyclopedia of Life Sciences Nature Publishing Group / www.Els.Net.. , 2001, 1-11.
18. University of Plymouth, Medicinal Properties of *Triticum Aestivum*. L: (2012). Effects of Freezing on Chlorophyll and Antioxidant Content of Aqueous Wheat Grass Extract,
19. Elmas Özeker (1999) Phenolic Compounds and Their Importance. Anadolu . J of Aari; 9:114-124.
20. Marja P Ka"Hko"Nen, Anu I Hopia, Heikki J Vuorela, Jussi-Pekka Rauha, Kalevi Pihlaja, Tytti S Kujala. *et al* (1999) Antioxidant Activity of Plant Extracts Containing

Phenolic Compounds. J Agric Food Chem. ; 47:3954-3962.

21. Manisha Vats, Harneet Singh, Satish Sardana (2011) Phytochemical Screening and Antimicrobial activity of Roots of Murraya Koenigii (Linn.) Spreng. (Rutaceae). Brazilian Journal of Microbiology; 42:1569-1573.

Assistant Professor,
Department of Biochemistry,
Marudhar Kesari Jain College for Women, Vaniyambadi.
Tamilnadu.

19. Hydrogeologic Evaluayion of Area Around Nokha, District Bikaner, Rajasthan

Priyanka Pandey and Mohit

Abstract

Nokha Tehsil of the Bikaner district falls in Survey of India Toposheets No. 45 E/ 1, 2, 3, 5, 6, 7 & 8, located between North Latitudes 27° 08' to 27° 58' and East Longitudes 73° 03' to 73° 50'. The area has arid to semiarid climate. The area suffers with extremes of temperature, i.e. high temperature in summers and very cool during winters. The topography is flat to undulate occupied by desert sand. The sand sheet conceals the pre quaternary geology of the area. The area is devoid of any hills. The area being a located in Thar Desert, the water is the most prized thing here. There is no stream of any notable significance; except for a few ephemeral rivulets. There are some water bodies in the form of ponds which supplies water for fulfilling various domestic needs of residents of the area. The availability of water in these ponds is mainly during rainy season and only up to some months of winters. Hence, the ground water is important commodity as it is available round the year. But it is available at depth and its quality is potable to non potable at different places. The important geologic formations of area are Bilara Group and Nagaur Group of Marwar Supergroup of Eocambrian period, Palana Formation of Eocene age and the Quaternary Formations. To evaluate the hydrologic status of the study area Ground Water data has been collected and various kinds of maps have been prepared. The study shows that the minimum depth to water is 34.55 m at village Mundar located in south-eastern part, whereas maximum depth to water is 116.40 m at Munjasar located in north-western part of the area. Depth to Water Table Map shows that the shallow depths to the ground water are present in the southern part whereas it is increases towards northern parts of the study area. The difference between the minimum and maximum depths to water level is 81.85 m, which shows a great variation in water level depths in the area. Since the ground water in the northern part in comparison to southern part is of better quality; hence its extraction is more than the ground water in southern part.

Introduction

The study area is Nokha Tehsil of the Bikaner district, situated in its southern part. The district Bikaner is a part of "Thar Desert" in North-western Rajasthan and to be found between North Latitudes 27° 11' to 29° 03' and East Longitudes 71° 54' to 74° 12'. The district occupies an area of about 27244 sq. Km. From the view of the administration, the Bikaner district is subdivided into 8 Tehsils, namely - Bikaner, Nokha, Lunkaransar, Kolayat, Dungargarh, Chhatargarh, Khajuwala and Pugal.

The Nokha which is also known as Nokha Mandi is a Town and a tehsil head quarter in Bikaner District. It is connected to the district head quarters of Bikaner and Nagaur by National Highway No. 89 and the railways. The boundary of Nokha Tehsil is co-terminus with boundary of Nokha block, located between North Latitudes 27° 08' to 27° 58' and East Longitudes 73° 03' to 73° 50' and falls in Survey of India Toposheets No. 45 E/ 1, 2, 3, 5, 6, 7 & 8. There are 128 villages in Tehsil Nokha and covers an area of 3767.67 Km^2. Important villages of study area are Nokha, Rasisar, Jasarasar, Somalsar, Mukam, Raisar, Himatasar, Badhnu, Kuchore Athuni, Kuchore Aguni, Masuri, Sajanwasi, Morkhana, Jaisinghdesar Kaliya, Sadhasar, Kakara, Morkhana, Sowa, Hiyandesar, Charakara, Thawaria, Jaisinghdesar Magra, Munjasar, Dharnok, Kumbasaria, Dhingsari, Nathusar, Panchu, Udasar, Kudsu, Kishnasar, Desalsar, Janglu, Jegla, Surpura, Manyana, Bhamatsar, Nokha Gaon, Kanwalisar, Hansasar, Kakku, Bhadala, Sadhuna, Sarunda, Chitana, Kedli etc.

The area of Nokha Tehsil of Bikaner District being part of "Thar Desert" hence has arid climatic conditions characterized by very low and erratic rainfall, high evapo-transpiration, high diurnal variation, prolonged summers, dry climate, scarcity of water, sparse vegetation etc. [Sharma & Shandilya 2005]. The Tehsil suffers with extremes of temperature and climate. It is dreadfully hot in summer and awfully cool in winters, high velocity hot wind in summers from south west which sweeps away sand and creates sand dunes and very cold breeze in winters from north which sometimes freezes the water available on the surface [Sharma 2002; Shandilya & Sharma 2004]. Almost all the villages have at least one tank in the vicinity that provides drinking water to the live stock and human being. The ground water is available at depth and its quality is either potable or non potable at different places.

The average annual relative humidity is 48%, but in the monsoon period its average is 55% [average varies from 46 to 63% in the months of monsoon period] in the Nokha Tehsil. The rain fall pattern of the area differs much in frequency, intensity and duration from rest of the state and the country. The monsoon period starts from July and ends in September, but the rainfall is very little and the average annual rainfall in this desert part is only 312 mm [Sharma & Shandilya 2005; Shandilya & Sharma 2005].

Geomorphology

The area has undulated topography occupied by desert sand sheet along with the shifting sand dunes of varying extent and sizes, which conceal much of the pre-quaternary geology of the area. The study area is devoid of hills and there are no rivulets or streams of any notable significance; except for a few ephemeral rivulets [Shandilya et al 2006]. There are few very small streams are of first to second orders which arise from elevated uplands near village Janglu and at some other places in the northern part of the area and flows to the lowlands in the central or southern part of the area, for a short distance and disappears in the depressions or fields with or without well developed outlet point (i.e. Nadis or tanks to harness the surface water).

All major geomorphologic units of the area are of Aeolian origin and are formed by blowing sand. There are mainly five types of land forms present and are classified on the basis of their characters. These are Aeolian Plain, Interdunal Depression, Dune Vale Complex, and Sand Ridge Complex. The Aeolian Plain is a most important unit in the study area, which found associated with the Sandstones of Eocambrian (Nagaur Group) and Tertiary age, Limestone of Eocambrian (Bilara Group) age and Alluvium of recent age. The Aeolian Plains are distributed mainly in the north, south and western part of the area but small plains are found scattered through out the study area. The Dune Vale Complex is the second largest unit in the area and found in all directions, but mainly in the western and eastern parts of the area. The Dune Vale Complex is characterized by undulations composed of number of sand dunes which are indicative of aridity of the area. The Interdunal Depressions are present in all parts of the area and characterized by shallow depressional area between two mega sand dunes. The Sand Ridge Complexes are found here and there in all part of the study area and there general extension is in NE-SW, which is the main wind blowing direction in the region.

Geology and Hydrogeology

The geological formations found in the study area ranges from Eocambrian (Paleozoic) to the Quaternary age. The rocks of Marwar Supergroup of Eocambrian period are represented by Bilara and Nagaur Groups and are underlain by Palana Formation of Eocene age. The Quaternary Formations overlies all the older formations. The Bilara Group of Marwar Supergroup is represented by limestone and found in the southern most part of the area around villages Sadhuna, Kedli, Sarunda, Indarpura etc. The quality of water in this formation is poor as the water is not potable. The Nagaur Groups of Marwar Supergroup is consisted of sandstone. It is found in the central part of the area and has extension from extreme east to the west. It covers about 70% part of the area and is a good aquifer. The Important villages' falls in the area of this formation are Nokha Mandi, Himatasar, Kakku, Rora, Kutsu, Panchu, Hiyantesar, etc. The Palana Formation of Tertiary age is the second largest formation. It is consisted of beds of clays, sandstones, etc. and found to occur in the northern part of the study area. The sandstone of this formation is a good aquifer in which the availability and quality of water is good; but quality of water is deteriorated in the clay beds. The Quaternary Formations are present throughout the study area. These are represented by alluvium, calcrete (mainly calcrete & gypcrete), clay, silt and unconsolidated sediments of gravel and sand. The recent wind blown sand found in the form of sand sheet and dunes that covers almost the whole area; hence the outcrops of all the old geologic formations are concealed.

The ground water is not available in this formation except the alluvium, found as a localized patch in the south eastern part of the area, where the quality of water is poor. The geological succession of study area is present in Table No. 1.

Period /Age	Supergroup /Series	Geological Unit	Lithological Characters
Quaternary	Recent to Sub-recent	Alluvium	Blown sand, unconsolidated Sand, Silt,Clay & Calcrete etc.
Tertiary	Eocene	Palana Sandstone	Sandstone, Clay, Gravel with occasional lenses of Lignite.
Paleozoic (Eocambrian)	Marwar Supergroup	Nagaur Sandstone	Sandstonewith intercalations of Shale.
		Bilara limestone	Limestone(Cherty &Dolomitic) with Shale beds

Table No. 1: Geological Succession of Nokha area along with Lithological Characters

Analysis of Depth to Water Conditions

To analyse the Ground Water conditions Depth to Water Table Map for Pre-monsoon 2021 has been prepared on the basis of the data collected from the field (Table No.2). The contours are drawn at the interval of five meters in the map. Study of the map (Fig No. 1) shows that the contours representing shallow depths are present in the southern part and the lowest contour is of 35 meters depth; whereas contours representing greater depths are present in the northern part. The greatest contour is of 115 meters depth located in north eastern part of the study area. The map clearly shows that the depth of the ground water is increases from southern parts to the northern parts of the study area. This map and Table No. 2 indicates that the depth to Ground Water levels in the entire area varies exactly between 34.55 m at Well No. 39 of village Mundar (located in south-eastern part) to 116.40 m at Well No. 16 of Munjasar (located in north-western part of the area). The difference between the minimum and maximum depths to water level in the study area is 81.85m, which shows a great variation in water level depths in the area (Table No.3).

Table No. 2: Static Depths to Water Level Data of Pre-Monsoon
2021

Well No.	Name of Well	Depth to Water Level (in m)
1	Badhnu	106.75
2	Kuchore- Athuni	96.00
3	Jaisinghdesar(E)	105.00
4	Lalamdesar	100.15
5	Masuri	113.00
6	Sadasar	98.00
7	Jasrasar	85.00
8	Sajanwasi	98.04
9	Kakra	73.70
10	Berasar	90.00
11	Morkhana	101.30
12	Sowa	105.00
13	Rasisar	81.21
14	Janglu	90.00
15	Jaisinghdesar(w)	105.70
16	Munjasar	116.40
17	Dharnok	92.50
18	Nathusar	95.00
19	Kumbasaria	95.35
20	Dhingsari	109.60
21	Udasar	114.15
22	Hiyandesar	105.61
23	Kudsu	107.00
24	Pannchu	98.10
25	Kakku	41.90
26	Sarunda	81.80
27	Chitana	73.35
28	Kedli	64.55
29	Charkara	68.00
30	Nokha Mandi	95.43
31	Somalsar	77.00

32	Raisar	60.75
33	Mukam	72.02
34	Himatsar	73`.00
35	Jareli	72.00
36	Gujsukhdesar	62.70
37	Thawaria	87.00
38	Jesalsar	41.21
39	Mundar	34.55

Map No. 1: Depth to Water Level Pre Monsoon 2021

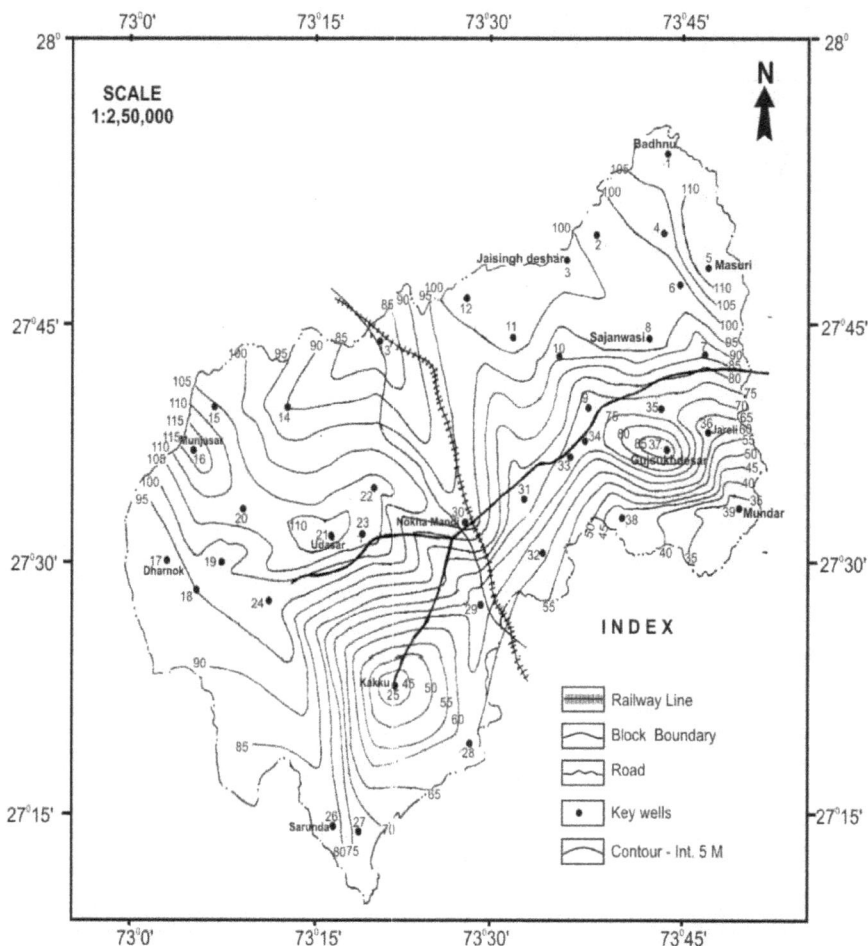

Table No. 3: Minimum & Maximum Depths to Water Level in Pre-Monsoon 2021

Min./Max. Depth to Water	Name of Well & [No.]	Static water level [m]	Difference in Min. & Max water level [m]
Minimum	Mundar [39]	34.55	81.85
Maximum	Munjasar [16]	116.40	

The study of the map also shows that there are concentric contours around Well No. 25 of village Kakku, located in the southern part of the area, where depth to water level observed is 41.90 m. The depth of the ground water is increasing in all the directions from this location. Another important area with a few concentric contours is around the village Well No. 37 of village Gujsukhdedsar, located in the south eastern part of the area, where depth to water level observed is 62.70 m. The availability of water is deeper in comparison to the surroundings, as the surrounding contours are of lower values from this location. There are some more areas with concentric contours around Well No. 16 at village Munjasar, Well No. 13 at village Rasisar, Well No. 3 at village Jaisinghdesar and Well No. 5 at village Masuri. All these three places are located in the northern part of the study area.

Conclusion

The area of Nokha Tehsil has arid to semiarid climate and suffers with extremes of temperature. The quaternary sand expanse conceals the pre quaternary geology of the area. The the water is the most prized thing here because of desert region. There is no stream in the area. The ponds (very few in no.) and the ground water are the prime source of water. Ground water is available at depth and quality is potable to non potable at different places. The important hydrogeologic formations of area are sandstones of Nagaur Group of Eocambrian period and Palana Formation of Eocene age. Hydrological study shows that the minimum depth to water is 34.55 m at village Mundar, whereas maximum depth to water is 116.40 m at Munjasar. Depth to Water Table Map shows that the shallow depths to the ground water are present in the southern part and the depth increases towards northern parts of the study area. The difference between the minimum and maximum depths to water level is 81.85 m.

References

Shandilya, A.K. and Sharma Shishir, 2004. Hydro-Meteorological Analysis of Bikaner for Climatic Classification, Oikoassay, Vol. 17, No. 1 & 2, pp. 41- 44.

Shandilya, A.K., Dubey Priyanka and Parihar Priti. (2016). Status of Ground Water in West of Nokha Tehsil, District Bikaner (Rajasthan), Geog. Aspects - Proc. 34th RGA Nat. Conf. on Envi. Conser. & Res. Manage., Vol.VIII , pp. 27-31.

Shandilya, A.K., Dubey Priyanka and Parihar Priti. (In Press). Ground Water Fluctuation around Nokha, District Bikaner, Rajasthan, *Oikoassay.*

Sharma, Shishir, 2002. Environmental Geo Scientific study of Bikaner and its Hinterland. PhD Thesis, M.D.S. University, Ajmer. 307 pp.

Shishir Sharma and A.K. Shandilya, 2005. Long Term Analysis of Rainfall Data of Bikaner for Hydro-Meteorological Purposes , Oikoassay, Vol. 18, No. 1 & 2. pp. 39- 43.

Assistant Professor,
Department of Civil Engineering
Sangam University, Bhiwara , Rajasthan

20. Water Pollution : A Modern Epidemic

Dr. Mahesh Kumar Nitharwal

Introduction

Pollution is a word that you hear almost every day in the news, at school and in day-to-day conversations. Our society has produced many kinds of pollution; some are more dangerous than others. Scientists are constantly studying how the different types of pollution affect the environment and how it can be controlled.

Among the Pollutions, water pollution is foremost crisis to be discussed. Water pollution is the contamination of water sources by substances which make the water unusable for drinking, cooking, cleaning, swimming, and other activities. Pollutants include chemicals, trash, bacteria, and parasites. All forms of pollution eventually make their way to water. It is the presence in groundwater of toxic chemicals and biological agents that exceed what is naturally found in the water and may pose a threat to human health and/or the environment. Additionally, it may consist of chemicals introduced into the water bodies as a result of various human activities. Water pollution is a major problem in the global context. It has been suggested that it is the leading worldwide cause of deaths and diseases and that it accounts for the deaths of more than 14,000 people daily. Comprising over 70% of the Earth's surface, water is undoubtedly the most precious natural resource that exists on our planet. Without the seemingly invaluable compound comprised of hydrogen and oxygen, life on Earth would be non-existent: it is essential for everything on our planet to grow and prosper. Although we as humans recognize this fact, we disregard it by polluting our rivers, lakes, and oceans. Subsequently, we are slowly but surely harming our planet to the point where organisms are dying at a very alarming rate.

Categories of Water Pollution :

1. Nutrients Pollution. Some waste water, fertilizers and sewage contain high levels of nutrients. If they end up in water bodies, they encourage algae ...

2. Surface Water Pollution.
3. Oxygen Depleting.
4. Ground Water Pollution.
5. Microbiological.

Sources of Water Pollution :

The key causatives of water pollution are:

- Urbanization.
- Deforestation.
- Industrial effluents.
- Social and Religious Practices.
- Use of Detergents and Fertilizers.
- Agricultural run-offs- Use of insecticides and pesticides.

Causes of Water Pollution
Pesticides

Pesticides that get applied to farm fields and roadsides and homeowners' lawns run off into local streams and rivers or drain down into groundwater, contaminating the fresh water that fish swim in and the water we humans drink.

It's tempting to think this is mostly a farming problem, but on a square-foot basis, homeowners apply even more chemicals to their lawns than farmers do to their fields! Still, farming is a big contributor to this problem. Fertilizers / Nutrient Pollution

Many causes of pollution, including sewage, manure, and chemical fertilizers, contain "nutrients" such as nitrates and phosphates. Deposition of atmospheric nitrogen (from nitrogen oxides) also causes nutrient-type water pollution.

Mining

Mining causes water pollution in a number of ways:

The mining process exposes heavy metals and sulphur compounds that were previously locked away in the earth. Rainwater leaches these compounds out of the exposed earth.

Similarly, the action of rainwater on piles of mining waste (tailings) transfers pollution to freshwater supplies.

In gold mining, cyanide is poured on piles of mined rock to chemically extract the gold from the ore. Some of the cyanide ultimately finds its way into nearby water.

Huge pools of mining waste "slurry" are often stored behind containment dams. If a dam leaks or bursts, water pollution is guaranteed.

Chemical and Industrial Processes

Almost all bodies of water in the world have some level of pollution from chemicals and industrial waste. Most hazardous liquid waste solvents, heavy metals, and radioactive materials are injected directly into deep groundwater via thousands of "injection wells.

Personal Care Products, Household Cleaning Products

Whenever we use personal-care products and household cleaning products, we should realize that almost all of it goes down the drain. Studies have shown that up to 90% of your original prescription passes out of you unaltered.

Sewage

In developing countries, an estimated 90% of wastewater is discharged directly into rivers and streams without treatment. Even in modern countries, untreated sewage can send disease-bearing water into rivers and oceans. Leaking septic tanks and other sources of sewage can cause groundwater and stream contamination.

Effects of Water Pollution

The effects of water pollution are numerous (as seen above in causes). Some water pollution effects are recognized immediately, whereas others don't show up for months or years. Additional effects of water pollution include:

The Food Chain is Damaged :

When toxins are in the water, the toxins travel from the water the animals drink to humans when the animals' meat is eaten. Dioxin is a chemical that causes a lot of problems from reproduction to uncontrolled cell growth or cancer. This chemical is bio - accumulated in fish, chicken and meat. Chemicals such as this travel up the food chain before entering the human body. The effect of water pollution can have a huge impact on the food chain. It disrupts the food-chain.

Diseases can Spread Via Polluted Water :

Infectious diseases such as typhoid and cholera can be contracted from drinking contaminated water. This is called microbial water pollution. The human heart and kidneys can be adversely affected if polluted water is consumed regularly. Other health problems associated with polluted water are poor blood circulation, skin lesions, vomiting, and damage to the nervous system. In fact, the effects of water pollution are said to be the leading cause of death for humans across the globe.Water pollution drastically affects human health; in fact, it can kill. In 2015 alone, a study revealed that waterborne illnesses caused 1.8 million deaths worldwide. It can cause contamination of drinking water – thereby contributing to waterborne illnesses.

Acid Rain :

Acid rain is made up of water droplets that are unusually acidic because of atmospheric pollution, most notably the excessive amounts of sulfur and nitrogen released by cars and industrial processes. Acid rain is also called acid deposition because this term includes other forms of acidic precipitation (such as snow).It contains sulphate particles, which can harm fish or plant life in lakes and rivers. Pollutants in the water will alter the overall chemistry of the water. Pollutants cause changes in acidity, temperature and conductivity. These factors all have an effect on the marine life. Marine food sources are contaminated. Marine food sources are contaminated or eliminated by water pollution. Altered water temperatures (due to human actions) can kill the marine life. Also, it can affect the delicate ecological balance in bodies of water, especially lakes and rivers.

Solutions of Water Pollution

We can all contribute to solving the water pollution problem. To stop algae blooms, Greenpeace suggests that we stop (or dramatically reduce) our consumption of meat, dairy, and eggs. Another solution is for farmers to repurpose manure into bio-fuels.

Reducing Nutrient and Pesticide Pollution

Solutions to water pollution caused by excess nutrients and chemical pesticides can be found in following broad categories:

- Encourage smart agricultural practices...
- Reduce urban/suburban runoff of lawn fertilizers and pesticides.

- Prevent further destruction wetlands, and re-establish them wherever possible..
- Improve sewage treatment.
- Reducing Sewage Pollution

As societies, we should place the same priority on upgrading out-of-date or under capacity sewage treatment plants that sometimes spew their contents into our waterways.

Water Treatment Process :

Following are the types of processes involved in the water treatment,

1. Physical Water Treatment Process
- Sedimentation
- Filtration
- Dissolved Air Floatation

2. Chemical Water Treatment Process :
- Pre-chlorination
- Aeration
- Disinfection

3. Physio-Chemical (Conventional) Water Treatment Process :
- Coagulation
- Flocculation

4. Biological Water Treatment Process :
- Slow Sand Filtration

Conlcusion

The problems associated with water pollution have the capabilities to disrupt life on our planet to a great extent. We must become familiar with our local water resources and learn about ways for disposing harmful household wastes so they don't end up in sewage treatment plants that can't handle them or landfills not design & receive hazardous materials. In our yards, we must determine whether additional nutrients are needed before fertilizers are applied, and look for alternatives where fertilizers might run off into surface waters. We have to preserve existing trees and plant new trees and shrubs to help prevent soil erosion and promote infiltration of water into the soil.

Therefore, water pollution is indeed a very serious concern because it not only has an impact on health and but also can have negative effects on various industries and agriculture. It is therefore highly important to devise methods to reduce the level of water pollution that we are currently facing.

References :
A. K. Dwevedi, Researches in water pollution, International Research Journal of Natural and Applied Sciences, 2017, 4(1), 118-142.
Z. Kılıç, Water Pollution: Causes, Negative Effects and Prevention Methods, Istanbul Sabahattin Zaim University Journal of the Institute of Science and Technology, 2021, 3(2), 129-132.
S. Kumar, H. M. Meena, K. Verma, Water Pollution in India: Its Impact on the Human Health: Causes and Remedies, International Journal of Applied Environmental Sciences, 2017, 12, 2275-279.
A. K. Pathak, Water Pollution and Treatment, International Journal of Environmental Engineering and Management, 2013, 4(3), 191-198.

Assistant Professor,
Political Science,
S.R.P. Government College, Bandikui (Dausa),
Rajasthan